Ancient Literature and Philosophy of Religion

Ancient Literature and Philosophy of Religion

Comparative Research in the West's Most Sacred Texts

Joel Steele

WIPF & STOCK · Eugene, Oregon

ANCIENT LITERATURE AND PHILOSOPHY OF RELIGION
Comparative Research in the West's Most Sacred Texts

Copyright © 2022 Joel Steele. All rights reserved. Except for brief quotations in critical publications or reviews, no part of this book may be reproduced in any manner without prior written permission from the publisher. Write: Permissions, Wipf and Stock Publishers, 199 W. 8th Ave., Suite 3, Eugene, OR 97401.

Wipf & Stock
An Imprint of Wipf and Stock Publishers
199 W. 8th Ave., Suite 3
Eugene, OR 97401

www.wipfandstock.com

PAPERBACK ISBN: 978-1-6667-3569-7
HARDCOVER ISBN: 978-1-6667-9304-8
EBOOK ISBN: 978-1-6667-9305-5

03/11/22

Scripture quotations marked ESV are from The Holy Bible, English Standard Version, copyright © 2001, 2006, 2011, 2016 by Crossway Bibles, a division of Good News Publishers. All rights reserved.

Scripture quotations marked KJV are from the King James Version with Strong's Numbers, public domain. Formatted and corrected by OakTree Software, Inc., Version 3.8.

Scripture quotations marked NRSV are from the New Revised Standard Version Bible with Apocrypha, copyright © 1989 by the National Council of the Churches in the United States of America. Used by permission. All rights reserved worldwide.

Some nations have prophecy, some have not: but of all mankind,
there is no tribe so rude that it has not attempted History.
—THOMAS CARLYLE

Contents

Preface | ix
Introduction | xi

1. Understanding the Ancients' Worldview | 1
   Parallel Gods and Characters | 5
   Parallel Cultural Phenomenon | 9
2. Classical Biblical Hebrew | 21
3. Theological Influence | 32
4. Textual Analysis and Historical Critique | 43
   Faith and Reason | 49
5. Literature and Theology | 59
   One Greater Than Jonah | 62
   Western Morality | 68
   Conclusion | 77

Appendix | 83
Bibliography | 85
Index | 91

Preface

THIS WORK EXAMINES THE parallels between ancient Ugaritic literature and the Old Testament. It briefly considers outside ancient sources to explain the connection between civilizations that exhibit parallels in various aspects of their culture even though they did not have knowledge of each other. It demonstrates that human civilizations have certain generic cognitive similarities regarding the structuring of their societies—offering an alternative to the trendy composite or plagiaristic theory pertaining to Near Eastern literature and that of the Old Testament. It argues that too much evidence suggests that each culture is capable of producing similar but independent cultural features. Therefore, it is a very real possibility that some of the god(s) and stories contained in Ugaritic literature and those in the Old Testament, which are associated with the same characteristics and actions as the Ugarit deities, are the consequences of a parallel phenomenon among two distinct and independent civilizations exhibiting cognitive similarities, which, in turn, have produced similar cultural features. Further, it may be deduced from these demonstrations that the Hebrew text has the ability, considering the vast number of resources within its own historiography, to be the primary source for determining clarification and accuracy. The second part of this study further critiques ideas regarding ancient literature and theology. It underscores the

Preface

procedures, methods, and theories used to understand humanity's past from two philosophical perspectives: historical and theological. Moreover, it offers insights necessary for proper interpretation of ancient literature.

Introduction

THIS STUDY BEGINS BY analyzing the first part of the West's most valued theological text, the Old Testament. It primarily argues against fashionable trends that claim the literature in the Hebrew Bible (Old Testament) is mostly a composite of various Near Eastern stories. This work was not composed with the intention of echoing scholars in the academy who have spent years reaffirming certain beliefs building their reputations to be compatible with long-held prevailing narratives, nor was it composed for the purpose of being well received by those in the Christian community. Typically, approval is extended only to those who have strong ties to the institutions that require a written confession pledging allegiances to certain creeds developed by the institution's transitory authority believing to be acting upon divine will. In short, this work was developed for those seeking a balanced approach to philosophical concepts dealing with the human condition reflected in ancient literature. Orthodox theology is sometimes viewed by the academy as inferior because of its assumed biased positions. However, the same could be charged to the academy for their unwillingness to accept any evidence that would seem to support theological positions—specifically those outside the metaphysical, paranormal, or supernatural. Whenever the phrase "orthodox theology" is mentioned in this study, it does not consider affiliation, denomination,

Introduction

or sect. For example, all three Christian affiliations—Catholic, Greek Orthodox, and Protestant—agree that Jesus was the Christ. Christ was sent by God to atone for humanity's sin. Christ physically died and was physically raised from the dead. They all believe in a Trinitarian God and that the Spirit is the only One in the Three who continues to occupy the earth (God and the Son are no longer physically present the way they once were in the Old and New Testaments). These theological concepts were extracted from Scripture. The objective here does not include advocating for the views of a certain Christian affiliation, denomination, or sect. Still, it's important to recognize basic established orthodox beliefs such as those mentioned above. The last point that will be made, before continuing with the introduction, is that this study will not be arguing that historians should accept theological beliefs pertaining to miraculous events as historical facts; they most certainly should not. It does advocate, however, that evidence derived from the historical record be considered regardless of whether or not it supports theological beliefs—providing the evidence is derived from a natural source.

The Hebrew Bible poses two primary challenges for translators. First, it is predominantly the product of an ancient oral culture that is far removed from our Enlightenment understanding of the world. Second, it is a document of faith understood by Christians to be the first part of the Bible—the Old Testament. Translators must consider to what extent theology should influence the translation of the ancient text.[1] Moreover, there are other deities, figures, and concepts from the region that have a striking resemblance to those found in biblical texts. The Ugaritic texts, for example, provide information on several deities mentioned in the Old Testament.[2] Comparative data between ancient Ugaritic and Classical Biblical Hebrew may provide support for certain elements of orthography when it comes to the origin of uncertain Hebrew words and scribal practices associated with Classical Biblical Hebrew. Comparative studies can be helpful as

1. Damrosch and Pike, *Longman Anthology*, 39.
2. Williams, *Basics of Ancient Ugaritic*, 15, 19.

Introduction

a supporting role between two cultures, i.e., more available data from one can sometimes clarify the fragmented pieces of another. However, comparative studies often get abused; the trend has been to charge cultures with plagiarism when certain characteristics are discovered to be similar to their predecessors. The evaluation of ancient texts in this study does not consider the historicity of the literature. The animated description of experiences and fantastic claims inundating their stories serve to understand the ancients' worldview. The concern here is not with the modern corresponding reality of these claims or if they actually occurred; this is neither an apology for religious views, nor is it a discourse against them. Rather, this analysis consists of a symmetrical approach that argues there is an overzealous attempt to connect parallels between certain ancient Near Eastern literature and the Old Testament. Select occurrences have been chosen within the historiography of ancient Near Eastern literature regarding these contumaciously constructed parallels. Consequently, this research will demonstrate that although Ugaritic and Hebrew literature exhibit a parallel phenomenon, the Hebrew writings are not simply the composites of their predecessors. This research also contains components of philosophy relevant to intellectual history, philosophy of history, and philosophy of religion. The procedures and theories used to understand humanity's past and the methods theologians use to understand the theology embedded within the West's most sacred texts are critiqued. The nature of this inquiry, as it relates to the latter section, will inherently require that certain interpretative methods be applied. Those who have knowledge of theological methods will recognize some of the practices used in this study. Certain methods within the field of hermeneutics were utilized, but it is hotly debated among scholars as to how these theories of interpretation, if they can be called such, should be applied. The decision was made to adopt methods within the hermeneutical field that have the strongest semblance of those found in historical methods. If the ancient view of the world is not brought to prominence while engaging with ancient texts, a modern worldview will likely distort any original meaning

Introduction

the author intended to convey. Thus, cautionary measures have been taken to understand the ancient world through the lens of these ancient authors—bearing in mind the authors' theological concepts had a major impact on their worldview.

1

Understanding the Ancients' Worldview

BEFORE ANALYZING AND COMPARING Near Eastern literature, much prudence will be found in making an attempt to understand how these ancient authors viewed their world. The ancients understood the past differently from modern historians, evident in their writings. They had a mythical view of space and time. They believed there was an eternal recurring cycle of events in history. The ancients were void of any idea of progress for humanity in this eternal wheel of fate. They told their history through mythical stories that should not be confused with fables. Fables were the work of fantasies that no one was expected to believe. Unlike fables, ancient myths had a semblance of truth. Often, these stories were regarded as divine or sacred and had relevant applications for their societies.

Debates have emerged on whether these ancient stories, told by their authors, were meant to be understood as allegorical or factual. This, however, is a strictly modern view of ancient narratives. The ancients did not view the world from a modern perspective. Moderns attempt to understand the world through observation and rational thought. The world, from a modern perspective, is detached and can be objectively scrutinized. Unlike the modern perspective, the ancients did not view the world as distinct or separate from themselves. Their world was animated—alive, willful,

Ancient Literature and Philosophy of Religion

calculated. For the ancients, floods, plagues, and various other naturally occurring phenomena were understood as the results of actions taken by this animated world surrounding them. Interpreting nature this way resulted in directly experiencing it. Thus, being part of the animated world connected them to an intellectual mediation for epistemological developments. The debate over whether the ancients believed their myths to be true is derived from an inaccurate perspective.[1] Historian M. C. Lemon argues that "they lived their daily lives within a mythical consciousness in the first place."[2]

Perhaps it should be understood that mythical stories from the ancients are more practical than factual: they succeeded in making sense of their experiences. Whether or not all elements of their stories are true is beside the point. For example, in the future, our present way of knowing may be superseded by a development that is unfathomable to our current thought process.[3] Whatever false mentalities are held in the current age regarding our understanding of the world, they should not be condemned from the vantage point of future generations. For the same reason, we cannot discredit the value of the ancients' understanding of their world. The ancients falsely believed that the sun orbited the earth but were still able to make accurate calculations regarding seasonal and celestial events.

The notion of causation, i.e., the operation of impersonal laws governing events, was absent. The ancients made no real attempt to understand events—mainly because that was irrelevant to them. Often, they would credit the gods for various underlying factors that occurred in their animated world.

Moreover, there was no concept of humanity's progress. Thus, time, for the ancients, would go around in the vast historical cycle void of meaning.[4] There was a cycle of regularities—daily, monthly, yearly events that would all return to the point where they began.

1. Lemon, *Philosophy of History*, 16–17.
2. Lemon, *Philosophy of History*, 17.
3. Lemon, *Philosophy of History*, 19.
4. Lemon, *Philosophy of History*, 22.

Understanding the Ancients' Worldview

Flood, drought, and famine were inevitably repetitive. They concluded that if nature went in circles, so did humanity.[5] Nothing of real value could be expected from the physical world, so they looked to the afterlife as something of value to be cherished, i.e., death would be their escape from the eternal wheel of fate.[6]

Around 500 BCE, there is a shift in mentality expressed by Hellenistic culture.[7] Although many retained the circular understanding of time, there was a shift from the mythical understanding to the philosophical.[8] More on this shift is discussed in the following "Axial Age" section.

The passing of time is an important concept for the Christian worldview. Christian theology has strong connections to the writings and prophecies of the Old Testament. The authors of the Old Testament viewed their world in much the same way as other Near Eastern ancient cultures.

Moreover, scholars have noted the parallels between the mythical stories of the Near East and those of the Old Testament. Some scholars claim that the Hebrews took the stories from their ancient Near Eastern predecessors and "sanitized" them by removing elements related to magic and polytheistic deities. A polemical theory was developed by Christian scholars that is used to counter pagan myths. For example, the Canaanite storm god Baal is depicted, in Ugaritic literature, as "riding on the clouds." Ugaritic literature pre-dates Hebrew writings.[9] The book of Isaiah, therefore, is criticizing Baalism when Yahweh is depicted as riding on a cloud. "Baal does not ride on clouds; Yahweh does!"[10]

Ancient Hebrew writings, however, reveal a distinctive thought process pertaining to human origins and the passing of time. While many scholars argue that many of these parallels could not have happened by mere chance, the fact remains, there

---

5. Lemon, *Philosophy of History*, 32.
6. Lemon, *Philosophy of History*, 24.
7. Lemon, *Philosophy of History*, 29.
8. Lemon, *Philosophy of History*, 29.
9. Currid, *Against the Gods*, 28.
10. Currid, *Against the Gods*, 28.

are some important dissimilarities. For example, all societies of the Near East were polytheist except Hebrew; the gods of Near Eastern culture had limits, i.e., they were not omnipotent; the Hebrews' God is depicted as transcendent—he is not part of his creation, but he rules it; and, most importantly, humanity was created in God's image, the exact opposite of ancient Near Eastern deities.[11]

Axial Age

The period from c. 800 to 200 BCE has been identified as the Axial Age by some philosophers. Before this period, civilizations were known for their mythical way of thinking, as described above in the Near Eastern literature. During this period, there was a movement away from the mythical and toward the spiritual. Starting around 800 BCE, certain individuals began to experience a certain self-awareness, unlike their ancient predecessors. In the wake of this awareness, they experienced a longing for liberation and redemption. Each moved toward this aberration through various avenues—nirvana, being in sync with the toa, or recognizing a single deity and surrendering to his will.

These avenues were diverse in their convictions, but they all had a common feature—each inquiry was beyond the entity of self—and as individuals became self-aware, they were forced to face their convictions on their own. Many withdrew in solitude to reflect and meditate on their convictions and then returned as a *possessor of knowledge* in the form of a sage or prophet. Whatever the person became, it had a significant impact on the collective whole within society—pushing it forward. Individual examples are evident in such figures as Confucius and Plato (although there are more). The point is: thinkers in China, ascetics in India, philosopher in Greece, and prophets in Israel all fit the core motif, regardless of their divergence in belief, content, or inner disposition.[12] This movement was not confined to a specific area; it occurred on

11. Currid, *Against the Gods*, 40.
12. Jasper, *Origin and Goal*, 10–11.

a global scale without one being aware of the other. It's important to note this theory, because it corresponds to the "Parallel Cultural Phenomenon" section of this study that is central to the thesis.

This awakening of the consciousness experienced by certain individuals enabled them to think deeply on the state of humanity. Theories were developed on the best ways civilized people could live together and be governed. Certain philosophers and prophets traveled within their domains, advising and teaching the core principles of their theories and insights. The period that experienced these developments (argued by some) cannot be dismissed as simply the progression of the human race. The highest thought potential expressed by these individuals did not become common for all. The rulers who succeeded these gifted individuals, for example, were unable to apply the creative principles that were passed on to them.[13] Nevertheless, it will suffice, for the purpose of this study, to consider these intellectual ideas within the historiography of world history as we navigate through this literary exposition.

Parallel Gods and Characters

Ugarit was a coastal city about 150 miles north of Damascus.[14] The city was destroyed c. 1200 BCE. Archaeologists have recovered many tablets from this area. The original publications of the tablets are known by the contemporary name of Ugarit—Ras Shamra. They were published in a collection and assigned a number in the form RS NM.nn (RS = Ras Shamra, NM = archaeological season, and nn = individual find number). Translated from the German original, this volume's most common used abbreviation is KTU.[15] Many of these texts from Ugarit demonstrate close parallels to passages in the Old Testament, revealing a shared cultural heritage. Mark Smith argues that "the overlap between the end of Ugarit and the emergence of Israel can be seen in their association with the

---

13. Jasper, *Origin and Goal*, 12.
14. Schniedewind and Hunt, *Primer on Ugaritic*, 5.
15. Schniedewind and Hunt, *Primer on Ugaritic*, 21–22.

Ancient Literature and Philosophy of Religion

name of the Egyptian king Merenptah.[16] The primary Ugarit texts that provide significant culture, religious, and linguistic insights are the Baal Cycle, the Keret Legend, and the Tale of Aqhat.[17] A list of deities has been recorded from the Ugarit texts. However, for practical purposes, only a select few are consider for this study. El and Baal will be the primary focus.

In Ugaritic literature, the god El is at the head of the Pantheon. אֵל (*el*) is also used for the generic term *god* or to reference the God of Israel in Hebrew. The spelling and pronunciation are different from the typical usage for God in the Old Testament, i.e., יְהוָה (*yahweh*). The alternative term for God in Hebrew, אֱלֹהִים (*elohim*), is a term used less frequently in the Old Testament. Scholars debate the root of the word *elohim* and whether or not it stems from a single origin—originating from Ugaritic, Phoenician, or possibly Akkadian. However, the relationship between the name used for God in the Old Testament and *el* or *elohim* is disputed. It's interesting that in the Ugaritic text, *el* never has the article, which is the same practice used by authors of certain passages in the Old Testament (Qohelet, for example, when he uses *elohim*). It appears to be an ancient term used for God (in Hebrew) that later fell out of common usage. It became popular during the exile when there was a concern for returning to ancient foundations. Job uses it frequently, but in the postexilic books (2 Chronicles, Nehemiah, and Daniel), it is used a total of only five times.[18] Moreover, the Ugaritic text uses epithets when referencing El, for example, "the kindly one, El the merciful."[19] This practice parallels with verses in the Old Testament concerning the term: "El of Knowledge" (I Sam 2:3); "El of glory" (Ps 29:3); "El of eternity" (Gen 21:33). However, the term is also used to denote Israel's deity: "El, the God of Israel" (Gen 33:20). There could be, however, a relationship between Classical Hebrew and Ugaritic literature when it comes to how this term was applied. Further, in the book of Ezekiel, the author uses not only

16. Smith, "Ugarit and the Ugaritians," 141.
17. Schniedewind and Hunt, *Primer on Ugaritic*, 26.
18. Harris et al., *Theological Workbook*, 43n93, "eloah" as God, god.
19. Williams, *Basics of Ancient Ugaritic*, 15.

the common term for a deity but names found also in the Ugaritic texts. The prince of Tyre is recorded as stating "I am El; I sit in the set of the gods, in the heart of the seas" (Ezek 28:2). "You are wiser than Daniel" (Ezek 28:3). Tyre is a coastal city south of Ugarit. A source outside the Old Testament compares the palace of Tyre to the royal residence at Ugarit.[20] In Ugaritic texts, Daniel (*Danil* or *Dan'el*) is described as the character who is unable to have a son. The deities are made aware of Daniel's situation and intercede; Baal petitions El, who blesses Daniel. As a result, Daniel and his wife are able to conceive a son, Aqhat.[21] This may be, some scholars claim, the same Daniel mentioned in the book of Ezekiel. This is because the author of Ezekiel associates Daniel with Noah and Job who were from the distant past.[22] However, scholars also argue it's not the same figure as in the book of Daniel, although it may be from the figure of this story in the Ugaritic texts (*Danil* or *Dan'el*) that the author of this book in the Old Testament (Daniel) takes his name.[23] Nevertheless, as will be explained in the section on "Disputes and Fragmented Conclusions," we find through cultural context and evidence provided by other Old Testament books that a conclusive solution to this problem emerges from theology itself.

Baal

The storm god Baal is one of the primary gods in Ugaritic literature. The Baal Cycle was extracted from tablets contained within the high priest's library at Ugarit. The tablets are incomplete and fragmented; what remains reveals Baal's rise to power with the defeat of Yamm, the sea god. Naturally, since Baal is the storm god, it's not surprising that, in Ugaritic literature, Baal is depicted as "the rider of the clouds."[24] Depending on the translation, a passage

---

20. El Amarna Letter 89, as cited in Smith, "Ugarit and the Ugaritians," 146.
21. Smith, "Ugarit and the Ugaritians," 160.
22. Merrill-Willis, "Daniel: Name and Location," 1249.
23. Smith, "Ugarit and the Ugaritians," 159.
24. Schniedewind and Hunt, *Primer on Ugaritic*, 25–26.

Ancient Literature and Philosophy of Religion

in Psalm 68 depicts the Hebrew God as riding on the clouds. The New Revised Standard Version (NRSV) translates it: "Sing to God, sing praises to his name; lift up a song to him who rides upon the clouds" (Ps 68: 4). The English Standard Version (ESV) translates it: "Sing to God, sing praises to his name; lift up a song to him who rides through the deserts" (Ps 68:4). The Hebrew word עֲרָבָה has a few possible meanings. The King James Version (KJV) translates עֲרָבָה in the following manner: plain (42x), desert (9x), wilderness (5x), Arabah (2x), champaign (1x), evenings (1x), heavens (1x).[25] The Hebrew lexicon on which many scholars rely—the Brown-Driver-Briggs (BDB)—translates it as "desert-plain, steppe," and in its earliest use, the word referred to the area near the Dead Sea.[26] For this particular verse, the KJV translates the Hebrew word as "heavens": "Sing unto God, sing praises to his name: extol him that rideth upon the heavens" (Ps 68:4). Translating the Hebrew word עֲרָבָה as "cloud" in English does not appear to be the best choice in this context. There are similarities between these passages, but word choice in translations may be a subjective matter. Nevertheless, as previously mentioned, the passage in Isaiah (Isa 19:1) depicts Yahweh as riding עַל־עָב ("upon a cloud"). It's debated whether this was polemical or borrowing (plagiarism). Baal is mentioned throughout the Old Testament. His elevated position among the gods discloses his ability to impact humanity by controlling a natural phenomenon, i.e., the weather. An example is found in 1 Kings 17 where a battle is shaping-up between the prophets of Baal and Yahweh's prophet—Elijah—over whose deity actually has the ability to produce rain.

Some scholars argue that Psalm 29 was originally a hymn to Baal. Supposedly, both gods demonstrate their power over the sea, although Baal was originally designated (by El) to be a servant to the sea. Other parallels include commissioning of grand structures to be built (KTU 1.2 I and 1 Chr 28:11–19) and motifs pertaining to the gods that transpire on a mountain (KTU 1.3 III–V and Exod 19:16–18). The God of Israel—Yahweh—according to some

---

25. See Psalm 68 KJV at https://www.blueletterbible.org.
26. Brown et al., *Brown-Driver-Briggs*, 787, no. 6160.

Understanding the Ancients' Worldview

scholars, displays characteristics so close to the gods El and Baal that Yahweh must be a composite.[27] Others, however, argue that these Old Testament parallels are polemics against Baal and the Canaanite religion. Considering the extreme of both positions, one holding religious convictions and the other with strong motives for providing alternative responses to religious scholars (perhaps because it contrasts with a presuppositional understanding, i.e., the enlightened world of postmodern thought), the debate is unlikely to be settled.

There is, however, a third option: cognitive cultural phenomenon. It is quite possible for two cultures to exhibit a parallel phenomenon regarding cultural aspects without any knowledge of the other's existence. Many paleontologists believe, for example, there are explanations for the mythological dragons in which various ancient cultures believed, e.g., the ancients' discovery of dinosaur fossils during their time.

Parallel Cultural Phenomenon

Adrienne Mayor is a research scholar in classics and history of science. Her work offers explanations regarding various mythical creatures that arise from antiquity. Classical scholars, ancient historians, art historians, archaeologists, and zoologists have long held the belief that many of these mythical creatures were imaginary composites of known animals. For example, the griffin—a combination of a lion and an eagle—was created (imagined by the ancients) for symbolic purposes. Mayor provides a compelling argument against such views.[28] She argues that the ancients' encounter with fossil remains, of unfamiliar or extinct creators, resulted in mythical creatures—folklore derived from naturalistic details. Mycenaean, Chinese, Scandinavian, and various other ancient cultures all have related depictions of giant mythological creatures with similar visual characteristics. Not all myths are

---

27. Coogan and Smith, *Stories from Ancient Canaan*, 15.
28. Mayor, *First Fossil Hunters*, 15–16.

fossil-related, and some mythological creatures are derivatives of previous myths encountered through trade.[29] Nevertheless, writings from the ancients attest that many of these mythological creatures were developed independently of outside influences, and some mythographers (Scandinavian) may have developed dragons and sea creatures in the absence of fossil remains.[30]

Moreover, similar structures built by ancient societies separated by a vast ocean and on different continents provide examples of like-minded cultures that were presumably unaware of each other's existence. The pyramids in ancient Egypt and the Americas are grand structures. Time separates the construction of these pyramids by more than two thousand years. The Great Pyramid in Giza is perhaps the best known in Egypt (Fourth Dynasty King Khufu 2551–2528 BCE). The pyramid age in Egypt lasted around eight hundred years. The Egyptians believed in life after death, and it was important to the culture for the pharaoh to be buried in a tomb enclosed within a pyramid. The pyramid would contain a network of chambers (with links between the king and queen) and air shafts that were "orientated toward the north pole star and the constellation of Orion."[31] Presumably, this was designed so the pharaohs could find their way to the gods. The pyramids in the Americas were used for a different purpose. In the ancient Aztec city of Teotihuacan, located a short distance northeast of Mexico City, is an impressive monument known as the Pyramid of the Sun (100–600 CE). Teotihuacan failed to develop a proficient writing system; as such, not much is known of its dynastic history.[32] However, excavations have produced the remains of many sacrificial burials, most likely human sacrifice (many were killed with their hands bound behind their backs).[33] Presumably, these sacrifices were to appease their gods. Regardless of the pyramid's purpose (Egyptian or Aztec), it is clear the structures are similar in appearance, despite the

29. Mayor, *First Fossil Hunters*, 27.
30. Mayor, *First Fossil Hunters*, xix.
31. Bahn, *Complete Illustrated History*, 104–5.
32. Bahn, *Complete Illustrated History*, 230–31.
33. Bahn, *Complete Illustrated History*, 231.

Understanding the Ancients' Worldview

two cultures being separated by vast geographical locations and time periods. The Aztec and Egyptian pyramids possess visual characteristics, but there is no evidence that the pyramids from the Americas are a composite of the Egyptian pyramids.

Likewise, visual adaptations from fossils incorporated into mythological creatures (dragons, among others) by ancient cultures is not an indication they are mimicking their predecessors. Human civilizations have certain generic cognitive similarities regarding the structuring of their societies. Furthermore, too much evidence suggests that each culture is capable of producing similar but independent cultural features as demonstrated by the existing cultural symbols—grand structures and mythological creatures.

Therefore, it is a very real possibility that some of the gods and stories contained in Ugaritic literature and in the Old Testament (which are associated with the same characteristics and actions as the Ugarit deities) are the consequences of a parallel phenomenon among two distinct and independent civilizations exhibiting cognitive similarities, which in turn have produced similar cultural features in their religions.

Cognitive environment criticism supports this theory as well by suggesting that Israelite literature is not exclusive to the culture of the Israelites but reflects many aspects of the broader culture across the ancient Near East.[34]

Moreover, similar features are observed in a study of modern literature conducted by literary critic I. A. Richards (*Practical Criticism*, 1929). Richards sought to demonstrate how subjective value-judgments were regarding literature. He presented his undergraduates with a set of poems, concealing the titles and authors' names. The students overwhelmingly celebrated the obscure authors' poems over well-established authors and their time-honored poems. However, it is the consensus of unconscious valuations that relates to this research. For example, the participants of the study were young, white, privately educated, upper-middle-class English people of the 1920s.[35] The residents

---

34. Walton, *Ancient Near Eastern Thought*, 11.
35. Eagleton, *Literary Theory*, 13.

Ancient Literature and Philosophy of Religion

of an area share structured beliefs and practices, producing similar cognitive features that are spontaneous, not composite; these students in the study each judged the literature on an individual basis, not as a group, yet they all proved to hold the same perceptions regarding the value of the literature.

The ancients' worldview may be esoteric, i.e., better understood by academics in specialized fields. However, the unexpected consequences from studies like the one mentioned above can be useful for understanding cultural features from any age. In other words, why wouldn't we expect ancient people from the same area, who share structured cultural beliefs, to produce literature that is similar but not derivative?

Similar to the cultures in this study that were separated by distance and geographical location—where giant mythological creatures displayed parallel visual characteristics—we find the same cognitive phenomenon in a virtual form. One of the two parallel concepts originated from the sixteenth century in Japan. The Jesuits discovered a Buddhist sect that had flourished since the thirteenth century. In an essay composed in English, modern Japanese Buddhist scholar D. T. Suzuki provides an explanation of the philosophy of this particular sect of Buddhism. Shinran (1173–1262 CE) was the founder of the sect, known as Shin Buddhism. Essentially, humanity's sins consistently surpass their ability to be virtuous and produce good acts.[36] Therefore, since each individual on one's own merit fails to consistently live a virtuous life, individuals are trapped in a continuous rebirth, death, and rebirth of the karmic world. This school of thought teaches that no amount of self-directed effort can ever be sufficient for one's salvation. The solution resides within Amida Buddha himself. Amida alone can save individuals from this repetitive cycle, but they must have faith in him.[37] The goal for students connected to this sect is to achieve the Pure Land paradise ("achieve" rather than "reach" is used, because this state appears to be more metaphysical than an actual physical location). Amida Buddha is equated to the

---

36. Jaffe, "Shin Sect of Buddhism," 2:75–76.
37. Bresnan, *Awakening*, 296–97.

Understanding the Ancients' Worldview

Christian God, sin to karmic wrongdoing, heaven to Pure Land paradise, and the Christian faith to Shin faith.[38] Fundamentally, the idea of Shin faith is that because individuals are karma-bound, and karma is connected with sin, they are, therefore, incapable of emancipating themselves. They must take refuge in Amida who awakens their hearts, and all ideas of self-reliance are purged. It is their faith in Amida that saves them, making them eternally his.[39]

This has an astonishing parallel to the doctrines of Lutheranism. Luther essentially proclaimed the same principles: humanity is by nature sinful, and no amount of good works could ever earn individuals salvation. Christ's atonement was extended to all humanity; all that is required is faith.

Again, these are parallels where the same concepts were reached independently from two very different cultures living in separate geographical locations.

A final point on parallel cultural phenomenon will be made here. A remarkable event in ancient Egyptian history involves the Egyptian ruler Amenhotep IV, who would assume the name Akhenaten. Akhenaten revolutionized Egyptian theology by establishing the first monotheistic religion, atenism. He accomplished this by phasing out all other Egyptian gods except the Aten. Atenism taught that Akhenaten was the Aten's son, who served as a mediator between God and humans. Egyptian historiography of this period demonstrates how iconography can be useful, i.e., during Akhenaten's religious reforms, iconography is absent of solar theology.[40] The point is, there are issues connecting Akhenaten's monotheistic religion with ancient Israel's. It is unlikely, though not impossible, that Moses was familiar with Akhenaten's religion. While this may cast doubt on notions of plagiarism or borrowing, it does little for promoting the uniqueness or the reality of the deity found in Jewish and Christian religions. At best, Yahweh and the Aten were both the inventions of individual unique human thought, i.e., of two distinct authors who shared a culture that

---

38. Jaffe, "Shin Sect of Buddhism," 2:76.
39. Jaffe, "Shin Sect of Buddhism," 2:90.
40. Greer et al., *Behind the Scenes*, 256–58.

Ancient Literature and Philosophy of Religion

influenced the creation of their gods. This does not create much of an issue for orthodoxy, because the historical-critical approach is not relied upon for a systematic belief system. However, the philosophical question of humanity's genesis comes into question, because, unlike orthodoxy, the historical-critical approach is the basis from which the narrative is constructed. While a critical understanding of history may raise the question of who made whom, orthodoxy holds that history is inadequate for truly understanding God (see ch. 4).

Not all parallels can be explained so easily as those mentioned above. And, while recognizing cognitive cultural themes within the ancient Near Eastern literature is important, it's also important not to mistake certain details within the literature as cognitive cultural traits. For example, the details in the flood story where Noah releases birds checking for dry land are similar to an older Near Eastern epic. The Gilgamesh epic depicts Utnapishtim (in a similar flood story) as doing the same thing—releasing birds from an ark to find dry land. The concept of a worldwide flood would have been a cognitive culture feature connected with the physical environment, i.e., the geographical area and the way ancients of the era conceptualized such natural disasters as floods, droughts, and famine. However, the details in the narrative regarding an ark and the release of birds is suspicious; it could be an indication of actual borrowing.

Disputes and Fragmented Conclusions

A recurring theme within the historiography pertaining to Ugaritic literature is that scholars claim it can assist in understanding the religious context of the Old Testament, although these same scholars will admit the Ugaritic tables are fragmented and pieces of various tablets are broken and missing. Two Ugaritic texts, KTU 1.47 and 1.118, were used to create a list of deities. From these sources, three primary gods emerged: El, Dagan, and Baal. The names for God in early Israelite literature—El Olam, i.e., God Everlasting, and El Elyon, i.e., God Most High—were used by some scholars (e.g., Frank Moore Cross) to argue that Yahweh was originally known as El but developed a separate identity.[41] Perhaps the use or absence of articles and epithets is convincing for some to conclude that the early name used to reference the Hebrew God, El, was a composite of the Ugarit god El.

However, as previously noted, scholars debate the root of the word *elohim* and whether or not it stems from a single origin—originating from either Ugaritic or other areas in Canaan. Indeed, there may be a connection as to how the term El is applied, but the relationship between the name used for God in the Old Testament and *el* or *elohim* is not conclusive. Further, out of the seventy Hebrew and Phoenician inscriptions found at Kuntillet 'Ajrud, in Sinai, dated from the ninth and eighth centuries BCE, one of them refers to God by his covenant name, Yahweh.[42]

In short, the evidence is insufficient for accepting the proposal that ancient Israel originally consisted of polytheism that eventually transformed into monotheism through a series of gradual refinements—resulting in a merger of various gods into a single God known as El or Yahweh (sanitized plagiarism). It could be just as appropriate to conclude (as many have) that the context and manner in which El is used in the Old Testament were to distinguish the true El (God) from the false gods that used the same name in other Semitic cultures (polemic approach). Both theories (essentially, plagiarism and polemic) are far from being definitive, and the issue is unlikely to be settled.

The final point on theism that will be made here is this: evidence exists in the Old Testament suggesting the Israelites did indeed hold to some type of henotheism (monolatrous) early on. For example, the commandment among the Ten Commandments in Exodus, that "you shall have no other gods before me," does not deny the existence of other gods. Some argue that the phrase used in passages like this one is referring not to not actual gods but to false gods (similar to a golden calf created for worship). Still others insist the passage is equating other gods to wicked or

---

41. Schniedewind and Hunt, *Primer on Ugaritic*, 18–19.
42. Martin, *Introduction to Biblical Hebrew*, 3.

Ancient Literature and Philosophy of Religion

demonic entities. These entities would have been considered false gods, and they certainly would not have been allowed to be positioned over the Hebrew God. Nevertheless, for most of the Old Testament, the authors' stance on deity is clear: Yahweh is Israel's one and true God.[43]

Some of the Ugaritic gods may be understood as divine children of El (Baal refers to El as his "father"). These gods are associated with natural phenomena, e.g., Baal, as previously mentioned, is the storm god. Baal's significance is evident in ancient Ugarit; only the palace was larger than the temple of Baal.[44] Many scholars have attempted to show that certain passages in Psalms were adaptations of a Canaanite psalm. It should be noted, however, that scholars have failed to produced convincing evidence that Psalm 29, for example, was an original Baal hymn. According to Robert Alter, "The same is true of the proposed linguistic and prosodic evidence that has been put forth to support the same claim."[45] The phrase "sons of God" has been used by scholars as evidence for parallels or reproductions of Ugaritic literature contained within the Old Testament psalm. The same phrase, however, occurs in other parts of the Old Testament as well. Are we to believe all the passages in the Old Testament containing the phrase "sons of God' are composites originating from this pagan hymn? More likely, the Old Testament passages containing this phrase are references to other celestial creatures (angels, perhaps). Essentially, the sons of God can be thought of as "God's royal entourage on high," as Alter argues. However, context must be applied, because the phrase can be referencing man or humanity. The storm imagery in Psalm 29 is perhaps how the poet of this Old Testament passage chose to imagine God's power—in a storm, not necessarily as a polemic against Baal and certainly not merely transposing a pagan hymn. Moreover, the mentioning of the primordial flood reveals God's eternal reign and his dominance over nature.[46] In short, linguistic

43. Arnold, *Introduction to New Testament*, 10.
44. Schniedewind and Hunt, *Primer on Ugaritic*, 19.
45. Alter, *Writings*, 81.
46. Alter, *Writings*, 82–83.

Understanding the Ancients' Worldview

and exegetical arguments, produced by parallel enthusiasts, have attempted to connect Psalm 29 with a hymn devoted to the storm god Baal—presumably influenced by KTU I.v, 5–39,[47] and KTU 1.4 VII[48]—are insufficient and therefore inconclusive.

The final disputed parallel that will be addressed in this section is regarding a well-known biblical figure. Recall our dilemma pertaining to Daniel—the figure referenced in the book of Ezekiel, the figure in the book of Daniel, and whether or not there is a connection to the character (*Danil* or *Dan'el*) in the Ugaritic texts, i.e., Daniel, the father of Aqhat. In the book of Ezekiel, it's interesting that references are made regarding wild animals, the desolation of land, and only the righteous being preserved. The author records God as saying, "Even if Noah, Daniel, and Job, these three, were in it, they would save only their own lives by their righteousness, says the Lord God. If I send wild animals through the land to ravage it, so that it is made desolate, and no one may pass through because of the animals; even if these three men were in it, as I live, says the Lord God, they would save neither sons nor daughters; they alone would be saved, but the land would be desolate" (Ezek 14:14–16). Noah was charged with preserving the animals during the flood, and Daniel miraculously survived the den of lions. Job's life was preserved because of his righteousness, but his children perished. The one thing that all these characters have in common is that they were all three viewed as being righteous before their God, Yahweh. This is the theological nuance that separates the two Daniels and perhaps discredits the claim that the Daniel mentioned in Ezekiel is the same Daniel as in the Ugaritic narrative.

References to Daniel in Ugaritic literature are found on three tablets, CTA 17, 19, and 20,[49] or KTU 1.17, 1.19, and 1.20.[50] This Daniel is depicted as a village elder who advocates on behalf of

---

47. Matthews and Benjamin, *Old Testament Parallels*, 266.
48. Arnold and Strawn, *World around Old Testament*, 157.
49. Dressler, "Identification of Ugaritic Dnil," 152.
50. Users with log-in credentials may search for KTU 1.7–1.20 in the image database of inscriptions and artifacts hosted by the University of Southern California, West Semitic Research, at inscriptifact.com.

orphans and widows. There is nothing spectacular about this Daniel when compared to the biblical Daniel. He is not shown to possess great wisdom, prophecy, or righteousness. Essentially, the narrative is a display of mercy by the gods. Daniel and his wife are not able to conceive a son. However, because of Daniel's prayers, lamenting, and mourning, Baal has sympathy for him and petitions El, who blesses Daniel with a son, Aqhat.[51] Scholars who connect the Daniel mentioned by Ezekiel with the same Daniel in the Ugaritic story do so on linguistic considerations. For example, the spelling of the character's name in the book of Ezekiel is different from that of the book of Daniel. However, the story of Aqhat in the Ugaritic text spells it the same way as in Ezekiel. Some scholars have suggested the spelling happens to be the same as the Ugaritic because the author of Ezekiel simply chose to use the traditional spelling of the name—as the name Daniel is well attested in different writings.[52]

Chronology is another issue to consider regarding Daniel's identity in the book of Ezekiel. From Ezekiel's point in time, the hero's reputation (Daniel, from the book of Daniel) would have been undeveloped; Daniel would not have been widely known. This argument is contingent on the dates of the books of Ezekeil and Daniel in the Old Testament. In contrast, the publication of Ezekiel's story must be considered. Some scholars have argued, for example, that the time elapsed between Ezekiel's developed story and publication of it (570–567 BCE) would have been long enough for the hero to establish his fame.[53] This claim may have some merit but not from the contemporary accepted dates, i.e., Ezekiel, 570–567, and Daniel, c. 539–165. Many scholars believe that Ezekiel wrote his prophecies in the sixth century BCE, in Babylonia. The book of Daniel attests that Daniel was taken to Babylon at the beginning of the Babylonian exile. However, scholars do not accept this date for the composition of the book. They believe that the stories were composed and edited over a long period. The

51. Coogan and Smith, *Stories from Ancient Canaan*, 34–36.
52. Dressler, "Identification of Ugaritic Dnil," 155–56.
53. Dressler, "Identification of Ugaritic Dnil," 156.

Understanding the Ancients' Worldview

earliest court stories are dated 539–333 BCE; these stories were eventually collected and merged with others to form the book of Daniel.[54] Scholars also believe that Ezekiel's followers edited and expanded his prophecies. Thus, there are discrepancies between the dates of each book for claiming that the hero in the book of Daniel is the same figure mentioned by Ezekiel. For example, what edited or expanded version of Ezekiel's work and the date of such can be compared to the book of Daniel's attestation regarding his reputation being established?

In short, the dating of most biblical books is no more than a rough estimate, hotly debated among scholars. Considering the wide range of dates assigned to various parts of composed material for the book of Daniel and the edits and expansions of Ezekiel, it is impractical to rely on dates regarding the issue of the character's identity, i.e., whether or not the hero from the book of Daniel is the same Daniel mentioned in Ezekiel.

The identity of Ezekiel's Daniel can be understood by examining the theological and cultural context. As mentioned, the one thing all three characters have in common is their righteousness. There is nothing in the Ugaritic text that would suggest that Daniel, father of Aqhat, was righteous. Of course, some scholars have developed, through speculation, fashionable arguments of special pleading depicting this Daniel as righteous.[55] However, these arguments lack the evidence to be considered plausible, and time is better allocated to arguments containing less conjecture and more credibility. In fact, it is extremely unlikely that Ezekiel would have considered the Daniel of Ugaritic literature as righteous, considering that Daniel was a Baal devotee. In contrast, the Old Testament portrays its Daniel as a righteous servant of God. For example, Daniel continues to pray and worship the only true God—Yahweh. When the king rushes to the lions' den early one morning, after having ordered Daniel to spend the night with the lions the previous day, the king calls out and asks Daniel if his God has been able to save him from the lions. Daniel responds: "O king, live forever!

---

54. Merrill-Willis, "Daniel: Historical Context," 1249.
55. Day, "Daniel of Ugarit," 178.

My God sent his angel and shut the lions' mouths so that they would not hurt me, because I was found blameless before him; and also before you, O king, I have done no wrong" (Dan 6:21–22).

It's clear, in the context thus far, that the linguistic, chronological, and distorted cultural dependencies, from which certain zealous parallel conjectures originate, do not demonstrate enough probability to conclude that authors of the Old Testament used other Canaanite stories as a pretext or even a model for their own. In this case, the theology attests that it was indeed the same person (Daniel) mentioned in Ezekiel as the hero (Daniel) in the book of Daniel, as opposed to the character (Daniel) from the Ugaritic narrative. This is because the author of Ezekiel would not have counted a Baal worshiper as righteous. Evidence for this is available throughout the Old Testament—Exodus 20:3, Deuteronomy 4:35, and Isaiah 44:6–8 are some examples.

The next chapter will provide an overview of the Hebrew language and its origin. Understanding the history of the language will be insightful and assist in recognizing biased arguments made by both sides of the parallel spectrum.

2

Classical Biblical Hebrew

HEBREW AS A SEMITIC language developed between the River Jordan and the Mediterranean Sea sometime during the second millennium BCE. The area associated with the language was known as Canaan. Different books of the Old Testament mention the language. An early written source, Isaiah 19:18, references it as "the language of Canaan." In 2 Kings 18:26, the language is called "the language of Judah." Later, Greek writers would call it *Hebraios*, and the Romans knew it as *ibrit*. The language was important to the ancient Near Eastern civilization that spoke it; but the language would become extremely important to Western culture in the future, i.e., Western theology would depend on understanding it correctly.[1] In its origins, Hebrew was exclusively consonantal, i.e., without any vowel letters. To clarify pronunciation, over time, Jewish scholars developed a vowel system, making notes around the consonantal text, which evolved into a vowel pointing system. The group of Jewish scholars who developed these notes are known as Masoretes. Essentially, they applied vowels to the text without (supposedly) changing the text or its meaning. By the tenth century CE, their work, the Masoretic text, became what is known today as the standard Hebrew Bible.[2] The Phoenician

1. Sáenz-Badillos, *History of Hebrew Language*, 1–2. Also, see appendix 27.
2. Roden, *Elementary Biblical Hebrew*, 14–15.

Ancient Literature and Philosophy of Religion

writing system, a continuation of the Proto-Canaanite system, is the ancestor of Hebrew.[3] Hebrew script has persisted for more than three thousand years.[4] The Babylonian exile marked the disappearance of the language from common use. Before the exile, in 587 BCE, the Hebrew script used in the prose sections of the Pentateuch, Prophets, and Writings is known as Classical Biblical Hebrew. Late Biblical Hebrew refers to the sections written after the exile. Classical Biblical Hebrew has survived "artificially" in the Dead Sea Scrolls.[5]

The Ugaritic documents discovered in 1929 led to an ongoing debate among scholars regarding the Ugaritic language and its relationship with other Semitic languages. In the majority of Ugaritic literature, unlike in Hebrew and Phoenician, the language was written from left to right.[6] However, scholars claim a valuable feature of Ugaritic, among many, is its preservation of most of the Proto-Semitic consonantal phonemes.

Scholars argue that other features have assisted in clarifying passages in the Old Testament.[7] For example, some Hebrew words are not fully understood because the meaning of certain Hebrew words may have changed or were even lost during the fifth and fourth centuries BCE, when the language nearly disappeared.

Further, scholars argue that some of these words lack context when the word is scarcely used, which make them problematic for interpretations. One example used by scholars to demonstrate this point is found in the book of Amos. Some scholars argue that the prophet (Amos) is referred to as a נקד (shepherd). Typically, however, the Hebrew word used for shepherd is רעה. The Hebrew word נקד occurs in only two Old Testament books, Amos and 2 Kings 3:4. Scholars compared Hebrew to other Semitic languages (Ugarit) and discovered the Ugaritic word that references a person who manages a large number of shepherds is *nqd* (transliteration).

3. Sáenz-Badillos, *History of Hebrew Language*, 16–17.
4. Sáenz-Badillos, *History of Hebrew Language*, 50.
5. Sáenz-Badillos, *History of Hebrew Language*, 52.
6. Schniedewind and Hunt, *Primer on Ugaritic*, 35.
7. Sáenz-Badillos, *History of Hebrew Language*, 32–33.

Classical Biblical Hebrew

They conclude that the transliterate Hebrew word נקד (*nqd*) must have the same meaning. Therefore, Amos was not a mere shepherd but a manager of shepherds.[8] Perhaps this is constructive comparative methodology. However, in the context of 2 Kings 3:4, would anyone mistake King Mesha to be a mere shepherd? In fact, English translations translate the Hebrew word נקד in this passage as sheep breeder: "Now the King of Mesha of Moab was a sheep breeder." Moreover, most English translations translate the passage in Amos to indicate he was not himself a shepherd: "The words of Amos, who was among the shepherds of Tekoa" (Amos 1:1). The Hebrew particle, the inseparable preposition בְּ ("among"), attached to the noun distinguishes how this nuance should be understood. Further, the Hebrew word is used in the plural in Amos בַּנֹּקְדִים ("among the shepherds"). Nevertheless, whether or not the comparative methods demonstrated here for understanding the Hebrew text are a constructive practice, in this instance, despite certain claims, they would not offer much insight to our understanding of Amos, nor are they likely to offer a new theological perspective or change currently held theology. However, arguments that will have an impact on theological perspectives are those that suggest there were errors that contaminated the text beyond recovery during the transmission process.

Transmission

According to tradition, from Moses to Malachi, the Old Testament Scriptures were produced c. 1400 BCE to 400 BCE, although most modern scholars date the earliest sources to the tenth century BCE. Nevertheless, to ensure preservation, the text had to be copied by hand. This practice of textual transmission continued until the fifteenth century CE with the invention of the printing press. The earliest production of the entire Old Testament in printed format

---

8. Schniedewind and Hunt, *Primer on Ugaritic*, 28.

occurred in 1488 CE. So, for roughly three thousand years, certain parts of the Old Testament were transmitted by hand.[9]

Prior to 300 BCE, textual transmission is obscure and complex. This is because as early books were recognized as authoritative, they were being copied and edited, i.e., going through the transmission process, while later Old Testament books had yet to be written. Further, some scholars argue there is evidence that during the transmission process, revisions were made to these earlier books. These revised books would continue to be copied in their revised form while the same book being copied by other scribes would continue in its original form (without revision). This suggests it was possible that there were two versions of the same book being circulated at the same time.

To add to the complexity, there is also evidence that these books were written and copied in a Paleo-Hebrew script that was replaced with "square" script toward the end of the same period. The letters between the two different scripts could be confused by a scribe. Therefore, both of these potential transmission errors should be considered in Old Testament texts.[10]

There was also an upgrade in the spelling with the introduction of vowel letters—*matres lectioni*s (mothers of reading). This upgrade occurred circa ninth century BCE. According to some scholars, the addition of vowels being added to the texts led to crowding, which caused issues in transmission, e.g., incorrect word divisions by scribes resulted in more errors. However, the Ugaritic texts confirm the ancient writing practices of Hebrew scribes. A small vertical wedge-shaped stroke in the Ugaritic texts would indicate a separation. By comparison, spaces were used to indicate separation in the Hebrew texts—evident in the biblical scrolls found at Qumran. It's not that word-crowding or "continuous writing" did not occur, but it was the exception, not the rule, among the texts.[11]

---

9. Brotzman and Tully, *Old Testament Textual Criticism*, 21.
10. Brotzman and Tully, *Old Testament Textual Criticism*, 22–23.
11. Brotzman and Tully, *Old Testament Textual Criticism*, 23–25.

Samaritan Pentateuch

The Samaritan Pentateuch (SP) consists of the first five books of Moses (the Torah). For the Samaritans, the rest of the Old Testament is not considered canonical Scripture. The Samaritans are a sect that originated at the beginning of the Israelite nation, according to Samaritan tradition. They claim to have upheld authentic tradition after the Jews separated from them in the eleventh century BCE. There is an ongoing debate as to when and why they separated from the Jews. An extensive survey conducted on Samaritan origins concluded that the schism came after the Jews returned from the exile. After the Jews returned, they were unwilling to accept the people of Samaria, who had remained in the land during the Jewish exile, because the Samaritans had not experienced exile and restoration. The Samaritans were best known for having their own temple on Mount Gerizim where they worshiped, instead of worshiping as the Jews did at the temple in Jerusalem. Archaeological evidence supports the Samaritan tradition regarding their temple being located on Mount Gerizim. Remains of a Samaritan temple were found on Mount Gerizim dating from the mid-fifth century BCE.[12] In the Gospel of John, the Samaritan tradition is alluded to via a Samaritan woman's conversation with Jesus in a Samaritan city (John 4:20–21).

At first, the SP was believed to be of little use for textual criticism, because the texts had been altered (most were copied in the fifteenth century) and none of the manuscripts was earlier than the ninth century CE. At Qumran, archaeologists found fragments that shared characteristics of the SP, but they lacked theological differences such as the temple being on Mount Gerizim. These scrolls from Qumran are referred to as pre-Samaritan.[13] Researchers noticed variations, rearrangements, and alternations

---

12. Brotzman and Tully, *Old Testament Textual Criticism*, 44.

13. These Qumran scrolls (pre-Samaritan) were not used as a basis for the SP. These scrolls are a by-product or similar to the Hebrew text used to compose the SP.

to harmonize certain passages that occurred in both the pre-Samaritan scrolls and the SP.

In short, many of the distinctive passages in the SP agree with the pre-Samaritan scrolls, suggesting that the SP reflects an ancient form of the Old Testament text. This means that the late alterations assumption is false. The SP preserved some older writings that are independent of the Masoretic text (MT). In cases where the SP and MT disagree, the SP typically agrees with the Greek Septuagint.[14]

Moreover, it is interesting that the Israelites were willing to give up the Paleo-Hebrew in favor of Aramaic during the exile, considering that Paleo-Hebrew was the script used to compose their early Scriptures when first written. Some scholars suspect it was because the Samaritans chose to preserve their own canon (SP) in the Paleo-Hebrew script.

Targums

After the Babylonian exile, Hebrew ceased to be used in everyday speech. Aramaic had become the lingua franca in Palestine, and Jews began to lose their knowledge of Hebrew. By the first century BCE, most Jews spoke Aramaic.[15] As a result, most Jews were having difficulty understanding the Torah and the Prophets when they were read aloud in the synagogue. Instead of creating a translation that would replace the Hebrew text, as the Greek Septuagint did, translations were given in Aramaic to accompany the Hebrew. These orally preserved translations were essentially paraphrases that became standardized in written form known as targumim or targums. Some of these Aramaic targums often deviated significantly from the Hebrew text, i.e., the translators were creative in their renderings.[16] There are scholars who believe that the Hebrew remains mostly accessible within the targums. Some evangelicals suggest that the targums were used by New Testament authors

---

14. Brotzman and Tully, *Old Testament Textual Criticism*, 45–46.
15. Arnold, *Introduction to New Testament*, 27.
16. Brotzman and Tully, *Old Testament Textual Criticism*, 78.

when quoting Old Testament passages. Theologically, it would be important to develop explanations that harmonize the misquotes made by New Testament authors regarding the Old Testament. However, the harmonization efforts would not be desirable if they unintentionally compromised orthodoxy. From a critical stance, the critic would need to come close to producing the original content—the original words of the author—before any original meaning could be extracted. This is a real challenge, and it is multiplied many times over when, from a critical approach, scholars begin to review the influence of literature surrounding the New Testament. The targums are not much use for textual criticism because of their paraphrastic and interpretive nature.[17]

Grant Osborne's *The Hermeneutical Spiral* reflects on Jewish exegetical patterns regarding the New Testament authors' understanding of the Old. Osborne mentions a quote by Jesus in Mark and how it was close to the form found in the targum of Isaiah.[18] There are some issues with this suggestion: the author of Mark, who wrote in a style of Greek (Greek may not have been his first language) which would indicate he was educated and lived outside of Palestine, chose to use an Aramaic version of the Old Testament from the targum rather than the LXX, when attributing quotes to Jesus?[19]

There are other problems with this claim regarding chronology and composition. Few scholars believe that the Gospel of Mark was written when Jesus was alive. According to critical scholarship, the book of Mark was written at least forty years after the fact; it was not composed as Jesus spoke the words. This makes it nearly impossible for Jesus's words to be recorded verbatim in the Gospel of Mark. So, if the targum of Isaiah was used in this passage, that could be attributed to Jesus, but we would have to accept that the Gospel of Mark was written during the time of Jesus. This is because if the author of Mark composed the book while Jesus was alive, it would make sense for the author to use the targums. After

17. Brotzman and Tully, *Old Testament Textual Criticism*, 77, 80.
18. Osborne, *Hermeneutical Spiral*, 324–25.
19. S. Henderson, "Authorship, Date," 1829.

Ancient Literature and Philosophy of Religion

all, Jesus and his followers most likely spoke Aramaic. However, the consensus among critical scholars is that the book of Mark was written anonymously, and it wasn't until the second century that "according to Mark" was assigned to the book.[20]

The identity of this Mark is also debated; e.g., was it the Mark who traveled with Paul or the Mark who was Peter's interpreter? Nevertheless, there is no serious challenge to the consensus regarding the date, and this is problematic for the evangelical scholar who approaches the text from a critical position.

Further, the source Osborne uses to connect Mark with the targums (Chilton) also argues that the base translations of the targums follow the original Hebrew text closely.[21] If so, it would be very difficult to connect that passage in Mark with the targums; it seems a single word was used to make the connection.

In short, the solution resides with the author's identity. If the critical scholar's view regarding the date for Mark is accepted, it is unlikely that whoever wrote Mark would have used the targums for attributing quotes to Jesus. If, however, more evidence is produced (perhaps someday it will be) that suggests the author, i.e., Mark, was recording his Gospel during the ministry of Jesus, it might make more sense to attribute the targum to this passage. A much deeper analysis could easily ensue regarding the source that the author used to compose Mark. Instead, this opportunity will be used to transition into the next section, for a discussion of how authors made use of previous texts as they composed their own.

Structuralism and Intertextuality

The doctrine of structuralism proper asserts that each section of any system has meaning only as it relates to the other sections as a whole. The imagery in a literary work, for instance, will have a relational meaning, as opposed to a substantial meaning. The relationship between these sections can be parallelism, opposition, inverse,

---

20. S. Henderson, "Authorship, Date," 1829.
21. Brotzman and Tully, *Old Testament Textual Criticism*, 77.

equivalence, etc. Typically, the method is analytical because of the failure to take the text at face value; overlooking the obvious meaning of the story, it searches for deep structures embedded within it that are not apparent on the surface. Similar to formalism, it brackets the actual content of the story and focuses on the form. Structuralism was an obsession for twentieth-century intellectuals, and elements of this theory are used by religious scholars.[22] The theory was superseded by poststructuralist schools of thought and new literary criticism.

The primary weakness in structuralism was its reductionistic tendency, i.e., the radical denial of intentionality. However, poststructuralist theories had problems as well with their developmental theory of multiple meanings embedded within the texts. Moreover, both of these theories moved away from objectivity of the text and what the author intended but toward the subjectivity of the reader. Some critics argue that the text becomes independent of the author as soon as it is written down. This claim has been challenged by emphasizing the necessity of understanding philosophical and historical backgrounds that enables the reader to correctly identify the intended meaning of the author.[23] All literary systems have managed to develop strategies for understanding literature but lack objectivity, and many fail to produce the intended meaning. The plurality of possible meanings is further enhanced when the focus shifts toward intertextuality. It's difficult to deny there exist commonalties within the text of biblical narratives, but there is evidence that certain parallel concepts were intentional.

Intertextuality, because of its theory regarding intrabiblical connections between the Old and New Testaments, is more prevalent in Christian circles. Intertextuality was introduced into literary theory by Russian critic Mikhail Bakhtin to describe the interrelationships of texts. Bakhtin argues that the text does not speak in monologue to the reader but through a series of intertextual exchanges that impact the text and its reception by the reader—because the author relied on various other texts to compose

---

22. Eagleton, *Literary Theory*, 82–84.
23. Osborne, *Hermeneutical Spiral*, 476–477.

the work.[24] Religious scholars have used this theory in conjunction with the Old and New Testaments to promote their theology.

Moreover, both Old and New Testament authors relied on their predecessors to further develop their theology. Examples are woven into various sections throughout this study. For instance, in chapter 3, the connection between Isaiah and Matthew regarding the descendant of David and the suffering servant or messiah is analyzed under the heading "Theological Connections between the Old and New Testaments." Also in chapter 3, symbols and projected imagery pertaining to apocalyptic prophecies are analyzed by comparing the book of Daniel and Revelation under the heading "Prophecy and Apocalyptic." Finally, in chapter 5, the story of Jonah in the Old Testament is arguably a quasi-mirror for comparative concepts related to Jesus as the Christ via a New Testament author (Matthew), under the heading "One Greater Than Jonah."

A final point on intertextuality regarding the Old Testament and Near Eastern literature is that many scholars have used this perspective to understand similarities between the two cultures. Scholars believe that the biblical authors were familiar with Near Eastern literature and made faint allusions to it, evident in certain themes and content, or they were using it to compose new work of their own.[25] It could be, however, as mentioned, these so-called allusions derived from their predecessors were not allusions at all, nor were they borrowed to compose new work of their own. Rather, they were produced from the authors' structural beliefs that originated from the authors' cognitive perceptions in relation to environmental features.

Orthodoxy in the Ancient World

Most of the ancient worldview consisted of a polytheistic system that was full of spiritual beings and gods. Erring on the side of caution, the ancients sought to hedge their bets. If, for example, a deity

---

24. Tull, "Rhetorical Criticism and Intertextuality," 166–67.
25. Walton, *Ancient Near Eastern Thought*, 15.

proved to be influential in human affairs, the community, typically at the direction of their leader, would seek to appease the god's anger. This is evident in the Ninevites' attitude regarding Jonah's message, discussed in this work's section on "One Greater Than Jonah."

Moreover, the temple was central to the community, because it worked as a mechanism for connecting divine order with human activity. Chaos was avoided when a god sat enthroned in his proper dwelling place, and stability could be preserved within the community. The temple was an earthly symbol of the god's heavenly residency. Religious practices and rituals had to be executed in an order of precedence to avoid aggravating certain gods.[26]

All of these descriptions could be considered ancient orthodoxy held by many ancient Near Eastern civilizations. Many of these characteristics can also be applied to the Israelites' God—a God who resides in a mobile unit for a time and provides precise instructions for designing the tabernacle (1 Chr 17:5; Exod 26:1–37).

However, Yahweh indeed had attributes that were clearly distinguishable from these gods. The Near Eastern gods were portrayed as sharing basic human traits. They were essentially no better than mortals, but they were stronger and existed longer. The gods were treated anthropomorphically in a sense, not necessarily in physical shape but being assigned the same nature, characteristics, and personalities as humans.[27] Yahweh, of course, according to tradition, created humanity in his image, but he was above his creation, not part of it; he was portrayed as righteous and, for the most part, did not display the same nature as humans. Moreover, as long as their position wasn't in jeopardy, the gods did not become jealous of other gods. In contrast, the God of Israel was a jealous God who did not tolerate this open-ended system. There was one true God; all others were false gods—a concept to which many Israelites had difficulty adjusting, evident in many passages of the Old Testament (Judg 2:10–12; Num 25:1–2; 2 Kgs 17:15).

---

26. Walton, *Ancient Near Eastern Thought*, 71–74.
27. Walton, *Ancient Near Eastern Thought*, 63.

3

Theological Influence

THOMAS CARLYLE ONCE QUIPPED: "Some nations have prophecy, some have not: but of all mankind, there is no tribe so rude that it has not attempted History."[1] Modern historians have suggested that Carlyle's phrase is too simplistic for the age of skepticism. His statement, however, is not only complementary to this study, regarding how different disciplines approach history, but is symbolic of the way ancient authors recorded the past compared to modern historians. Historical methods, used by historians, consist of analyzing and constructing fragments (examples include but are not limited to ancient tablets, scrolls, papyri, variations in ancient records, artifacts, etc.) while considering cultural influence and norms on the chosen civilization under review. Once the fragmented sources are analyzed, the sources found to be the most reliable (typically compared with outside sources) are deliberated in consideration of cultural traditions. A narrative is then developed, filling in gaps based on the aggregated historical evidence to produce an interpretation of the past. Essentially, historians tell us their interpretation of the past based on surviving fragments and cultural traditions that are used to construct a narrative of what most likely happened.

It is important to note the limits of recording and reconstruction of the past; even the recording of Scripture does not escape the

1. Breisach, *Historiography*, 1.

Theological Influence

human element. Moreover, there exist a multitude of various interpretations of the past. Occasionally, these interpretations contain slight differences, and at other times, they are dramatically different. Hence, a vigorous debate among scholars is unavoidable, and some claim necessary, for the discipline of history.[2]

Like the historical-critical method, studying ancient literature in its proper context requires a specific approach. This can be especially useful when it comes to literature related to religion or theology. In addition to translating a given ancient language to any given modern language, the historical-cultural aspects embedded within the literature must be considered. Critical analysis includes understanding the relationship between a society's recorded history, its literature, and the literature's original meaning, similar to the critical methods used by modern historians.

There is a distinction between the ancient Near Eastern view of history and the modern view of history. Typically, modern historians reflect on the past and attempt to extract meaning as such meaning passes in a linear fashion from the past to present to future.[3] In contrast, as previously mentioned, many ancient Near Eastern authors viewed history as cyclical. This, along with the inability to recognize a purpose—a linear progression toward an end—explains the fantastic claims embedded within their recorded history—if that history can be viewed as such.

Nevertheless, Christian orthodoxy holds that certain authors of the Old Testament recognize that "God's history is a providentially ordered whole in that different books from different time periods work together to reveal God working sovereignly to bring about his purpose in history."[4] This is a religious claim that resonates more with the philosophy of religion than with history proper, and it cannot be evaluated critically. Philosophy of religion addresses issues of this nature (reality) from purely a philosophical lens. Further, theological assumptions, as they relate to reality, are taken for granted. In other words, theological claims do not adhere

---

2. Brundage, *Going to the Sources*, 3.
3. Breisach, *Historiography*, 3.
4. Köstenberger and Patterson, *Invitation to Biblical Interpretation*, 161.

to the same standards as science—which we use to understand our known reality. The metaphysical, supernatural, and miraculous are all assumed by those making religious claims. Theology is an imperfect discipline used to understand God. Likewise, history is an imperfect discipline used to understand our past, based on our understanding of known reality—through scientific methods.

Old Testament Canon

In an effort to stabilize the contents of the Old Testament, an official list of authoritative books, the canon, was a gradual process, with no explicit account of the process. There are, however, several criteria that appear to have informed it. Two primary factors for a book to be deemed canon were language and antiquity. Many of the books considered as Scripture, for example, had been written in Greek or originally in Hebrew. The other requirement for a book to have been considered as Scripture is that it should have been composed no later than the mid-fifth century BCE. This was during the time of Ezra—the last person thought to have been inspired by God.[5] In early Hebrew and Greek manuscripts, Ezra and Nehemiah consisted of a single book, but later Christian tradition separated them, forming two books.[6]

Nevertheless, canonical interpretation considers the history of textual formation, which testifies to God and his plan for humanity revealed in Scripture. This means, according to theologians, the interpreter places emphasis on "the history of the text, its theological purpose, its distinctive theological themes, and so on,"[7] while acknowledging that these features bind the books together.

Moreover, as a whole, for the interpreter, the text should read as a theological document more than a historical document (although many historical accounts have been verified). According to religious scholars, the reading of the Old Testament should be

---

5. Coogan, *Old Testament*, 7–8.
6. Eskenazi, "Ezra: Name and Location," 675.
7. Köstenberger, and Patterson, *Invitation to Biblical Interpretation*, 159.

Theological Influence

theocentric, recognizing it as God's revelation.[8] Essentially, the Old Testament and New Testament relationship begins to materialize when the reader is aware of the theological theme connecting the two, i.e., God's plan for humanity's redemption through Christ.

This view, of course, is held by orthodox Christian theologians. Naturally, once the analysis turns toward the metaphysical elements in the narrative, it becomes difficult for the critical historian to evaluate. Moreover, viewing the texts this way, i.e., as a connected whole, requires a quasi-structuralist or formalist approach. For example, those practicing the Jewish faith will not see the connection between the Old and New Testaments.

Theological Connections between the Old and New Testaments

In the Old Testament, it is clear that the story of redemption—the promise of a new covenant—had been left unfinished. God's promise to save Israel and the world by crushing the serpent had yet to materialize. The New Testament claims that the promise of a kingdom, revealed in the Old Testament, was fulfilled through Jesus Christ's death and resurrection.[9] Being aware of theological connections between both sacred texts is important to many theologians when it comes to interpreting and communicating the theological relationship between the Old and New Testaments.

The following example will be used to demonstrate theological connections between the Old and New Testaments. According to Isaiah, salvation hinged on the promise of a new David. The promise of a new David relates to the covenant with King David.[10] This new David would come from a descendant of King David: "A shoot will come up from the stump of Jesse, and a branch shall grow out of his roots" (Isa 11:1). Isaiah proclaims that the one who is coming will establish peace and reign from the throne of David

---

8. Köstenberger and Patterson, *Invitation to Biblical Interpretation*, 157–58.
9. Schreiner, *King in His Beauty*, 428.
10. Schreiner, *King in His Beauty*, 334.

(Isa 9:6–7). The books of Matthew and Luke record the genealogy of Jesus. There is a minor discrepancy between them regarding who Joseph's father was,[11] but the point is made clear regarding the genealogy of Jesus: he was a descendant from David. The lineage is traced through Joseph, who was Jesus's earthly father: "Obed the father of Jesse, and Jesse the father of King David . . . and Jacob the father of Joseph, the husband of Mary, of whom was born Jesus, who is called Christ" (Matt 1:5–6, 16). Here we have a theological connection between the book of Isaiah and the way the New Testament portrays Jesus. Moreover, the decision made by the author(s) to include a genealogy that portrays Jesus as the offspring of David was influenced by Old Testament prophesy.

Isaiah describes the new David as "Wonderful Counselor, Mighty God, Everlasting Father, Prince of Peace" (Isa 9:6), making it evident he is more than simply a descendant of David. The first part of the sentence in Isaiah 9:6 proclaims: "For us a child is born."

However, the coming of such a king was not fulfilled in Isaiah's time. In Isaiah 7, there is an interesting passage: "The virgin will be with child and give birth to a son, and will call him Immanuel" (Isa 7:14). Once again, the theological theme of Isaiah is seen in two of the Synoptic Gospels, Matthew and Luke. "She [Mary] will give birth to a son, and you are to give him the name Jesus, because he will save his people from their sins" (Matt 1:21). In the next verse, the author acknowledges that this was to fulfill the prophecy in Isaiah 7:14. Likewise, the same references are found in Luke. An angel was sent by God to inform Mary, "a virgin pledged to be married to a man named Joseph, a descendant of David," that God had found favor with her and she would become pregnant (Luke 1:26–27).

In this comparison, Jesus is portrayed by the New Testament, as prophesied by the book of Isaiah, as not only having a miraculous conception but as being divine from birth. The description provided in Isaiah 9:6 regarding the coming of the new David is

---

11. For an explanation on the discrepancy regarding Joseph's father, see Eusebius, *Church History*, bk 1, 35–37.

Theological Influence

regarding a deity. The author assigns the title "Mighty God" and "Everlasting Father" in the passage to describe the new David.

Although the prophet does not state it explicitly, Christians who have a canonical and theological bias will compare the passages in Isaiah with those in John that clearly view Jesus as God. Isaiah 53:1 is referenced in John 12:38. Further, other passages in John disclose that Jesus and God are one and the same. For example, when the Pharisees challenge his authority, Jesus states, "If you knew me, you would know my Father also" (John 8:19).

Another Old Testament passage that appears to have had a major theological connection with the New Testament is also found in the book of Isaiah. Isaiah 53 seems to be one of the best sources that can be compared with how the New Testament portrays Jesus theologically: "They made his grave with the wicked and his tomb with the rich, although he had done no violence, and there was no deceit in his mouth. Yet it was the will of the LORD to crush him with pain. When you make his life an offering for sin, he shall see his offspring, and shall prolong his days; through him the will of the Lord will shall prosper" (Isa 53:9–10). This prophecy is evident throughout the New Testament by the way Jesus lived—without sin—innocent. Yet, it was God's will for him to be the offering in place of the guilty, according to orthodox theology. Moreover, Jesus was crucified with "the wicked," assigned a grave with them, but was buried with the rich in a grave supplied by Joseph of Arimathea, clearly fulfilling the first half of the prophesy in verse nine.

There are passages in the same chapter of Isaiah that have theological connections to passages in other parts of the New Testament. For example, "But he was pierced for our transgressions, he was crushed for our iniquities; the punishment that brought us peace was upon him, and by his wounds we are healed" (Isa 53:5). This passage may have influenced the passage in John where one of the soldiers pierced Jesus's side (John 19:34), although the Johnanine passage is attributed to Exodus, Numbers, and Psalms, regarding the prophesy "not one of his bones will be broken" (John 19:36–37). Still, Isaiah clearly influenced John to portray Jesus as

Ancient Literature and Philosophy of Religion

the sacrificial Lamb: "He was led like a lamb to the slaughter" (Isa 53:7). The prophecy begins to materialize in the first chapter of John, when John proclaims, "Look, the Lamb of God, who takes away the sins of the world!" (John 1:29). Moreover, many Christians believe that the end of Isaiah 53 makes it clear that the suffering servant was Jesus: "For he bore the sin of many, and made intercession for the transgressors." Evident in the Gospel of John, Jesus testifies that God was the one who sent the servant, because he loved the world and those that believed would not be condemned but saved through him, fulfilling God's plan (John 3:16–17).

Theologians believe that viewing the Old and New Testaments as sacred canonized Scripture rather than strictly a historical account of events will assist the reader with a more accurate interpretation of the theology.

Some elements within the texts can still be examined through critical scholarship by using different methods. For example, bracketing any notions of paranormal or metaphysical elements related to religious claims, the texts are evaluated by historians. Historians, however, are not concerned with theology or fantastic claims; their only concern is what can be established using the physical evidence. Prophecy eliminates much of the historians' critique regarding connections between the Old and New Testaments, because it is outside the physical nature of reality. A critical review of these passages shows that the New Testament author is composing his material in step with the Old Testament prophecies.

Genre

There are many genres in Biblical literature—prophecy, apocalyptic, narrative, wisdom literature, etc. Each of these genres can be considered "theological history" designed to teach a lesson.[12] Certain characteristics of each genre allow the reader to determine to what category a biblical passage belongs. For example, narratives exist in dramatic form, that is, stories. These stories typically

---

12. Köstenberger and Patterson, *Invitation to Biblical Interpretation*, 242.

Theological Influence

present historical accounts of dialogues and speeches that make up the full story.[13] Like other skills required for practicing theology, being sensitive to the genre allows the theologian to understand and interpret the meaning of text more accurately.

As previously mentioned, these biblical stories or myths are not the same as fables. Thus, in their own way they can be considered history: this was how the ancients made sense of their world.

Archaeology has validated many of the characters, events, and places mentioned in the biblical narratives. Beyond the dramatic and often sensationalized events contained within these narratives there exists an underlying message.

Moreover, other than the theological element, this style used to communicate historical narratives was not exclusive to biblical authors. For example, Thucydides took a similar approach when writing his historical narrative of the Peloponnesian War, i.e., he had historical actors delivering speeches to reveal their intentions. Modern historians doubt that these speeches ever occurred, and even if they did, Thucydides would not have been able to remember all the details. Nevertheless, an underlying reason emerges from these questionable speeches, providing the reader with details and causes of the war.[14]

Likewise, in the dramatic narratives of biblical literature, there is an underlying message related to the human condition, redemption, and certain attributes of God. These messages are often contained in prophecy or apocalyptic genres that sometimes converge or transcend, loosely speaking, from the Old Testament to the New. Examples are provided in the following sections.

Prophecy and Apocalyptic

Prophecy and apocalyptic genres share some of the same characteristics—symbolic images and language, visionary accounts or dreams, otherworldly mediators, etc. Both are "a revelatory means

---

13. Köstenberger and Patterson, *Invitation to Biblical Interpretation*, 237–39.

14. Gilderhus, *History and Historians*, 17.

of communication."¹⁵ The books of Daniel and Revelation are a case in point. These books deal with both prophecy and apocalyptic genres. In chapter 7, Daniel describes his vision and dream. There are four beasts that represent four kingdoms, or kings, who rule over the world. They are depicted as beasts because of the cruelty and devastation they inflict upon humanity.¹⁶ Likewise, in Revelation 13, a beast is described as being given authority to make war and reign over the earth (Rev 13:7–8). A theological message emerges in Daniel (ch. 7) and Revelation (ch. 13), which can be summed up in the following: regardless of how chaotic and evil the world becomes, redemption is made available for humanity by God (through Jesus Christ, in the NT). This entails that God is ultimately in control. The foreshadowing of things to come in Revelation discloses the same theological message, i.e., authority is given to evil powers for a limited time, but God will send his Son again for a final judgment.

In the book of Daniel, the vision of the beast is given a complex form in that it is not one beast but four. In accordance with the interpretation provided within the book for the character of Daniel, some scholars believe that these concepts represent a series of world stages and four empires of world history. Moreover, the appearance of a smaller horn that uproots the other horns represents a wickedness that extends beyond its predecessors. The application of this vision serves to disclose the destructive nature this beast inflicts upon the earth. Further, it reveals the worst and last tyrant's fate: he is judged and sentenced by God.¹⁷

The theological message here in Daniel seems to be revealing a prophecy regarding earthly kingdoms that will wage war and persecute God's people. However, this will be allowed only for a certain time before the kingdom of God comes to earth and pronounces judgment in favor of the saints. The fourth and final beast, or kingdom, will be destroyed by God, and God will then hand authority over to his people. God's kingdom will last for eternity,

---

15. Köstenberger and Patterson, *Invitation to Biblical Interpretation*, 520.
16. Schreiner, *King in His Beauty*, 392.
17. Beasley-Murray, "Interpretation of Daniel 7," 45.

Theological Influence

and all will worship and obey him (Dan 7:17–26). This prophecy is consistent with events in the Gospels. Jesus is the Son of Man, who came to free his people from the sins of the world. He accomplished this through his death and resurrection. Thus, the serpent and his beastly kingdoms that inflict suffering on humanity were defeated by Christ. Moreover, the saints share in Christ's victory as long as they are united with him.[18]

The same theological motif and pattern is found in Revelation. The beasts in Revelation chapter 13, like the beast in Daniel chapter 7, are given power to make war with the saints, and both visions depict a beast as emerging from particular places (from the sea, in Daniel; one from the sea, another from the earth, in Revelation). For Christians, the prophecy from Daniel materialized in the New Testament, specifically, in the Gospels, regarding Christ's atonement. However, John's prophecy was much later than Christ's atonement, positioned at the end of the Bible and perhaps written CE 81–96.[19]

There are many theories as to who or what the beasts are in the book of Revelation. For Hippolytus, they were the Roman Empire; others believed they were Nero or Domitian. In the sixteenth century, Luther believed the sea-beast described in Revelation to be the Germanic Holy Roman Empire, and the papacy to be the earth-beast.[20] It seems that every age has its beasts. However, there does seem to be a consensus regarding the attributes of this evil, i.e., it appears to be a worldly power and possibly a false prophet or a combination of such, manifested in the symbolic image of the beast from the sea and the beast from the earth. Precisely whoever or whatever they are, clearly, their authority was given to them by God. The author strongly emphasizes this, as it is mentioned no less than four times in Revelation 13.[21] Hence, God has ultimate authority, even in the chaotic times described here by John.

---

18. Schreiner, *King in His Beauty*, 393.
19. G., "Editorial," 5.
20. G., "Editorial," 6–8.
21. Schreiner, *King in His Beauty*, 620.

Ancient Literature and Philosophy of Religion

Modern interpretations of the sea-beast seem to think it is the general influence of the world—the influencer of this world who opposes God, i.e., Satan. The earth-beast, according to some modern theories, symbolizes the false religions and philosophies of the world.[22] Nonetheless, those who side with the two beasts will be destroyed by Christ in the end.

Parallels in Scripture

In the book of Romans, we learn that God has established authorities and governments on earth. "Everyone must submit himself to the governing authorities, for there is no authority except that which God has established. The authorities that exist have been established by God" (Rom 13:1). Here we have a passage in Scripture that parallels, in regard to meaning, with the passages in Revelation: "He [the sea-beast] was given power to make war against the saints and to conquer them" (Rev 13:7). In the same two parallel passages, there also exists a pattern. As previously stated, the author of Revelation mentions four times that the authority and power of the beasts comes from God. This same repetitiveness is seen in Romans 13 regarding the source of authority on earth.

In the book of Isaiah, a description of the Lord's entrance onto earth is provided: "See, the Lord rides on a swift cloud and is coming to Egypt" (Isa 19:1). Likewise, in the book of Daniel, Daniel describes the image that resembles "the son of man" entering with the clouds: "In my vision at night I looked, and there before me was one like a son of man, coming with the clouds of heaven" (Dan 7:13). Further, in Revelation, it is Jesus whose second coming via the clouds is anticipated. In Daniel, the reign of God will be, and was established, through the "son of man."[23] The same prophecy and apocalyptic theme occurs within the narrative of Revelation: it is Christ who will establish his kingdom on earth in the final days.

---

22. G., "Editorial," 18–19.
23. Schreiner, *King in His Beauty*, 620.

4

Textual Analysis and Historical Critique

CHRISTOLOGY, DEFINED AS THE theological interpretation of the person and work of Christ, corresponds to theologians who consider historical practice to be a secondary element within their discipline. Philosophy, for example, is relied on by theologians but only to the extent that it can assist in clarifying their theology. It is faith based on Scripture that is central to the discipline of Christian theology. History and philosophy are secondary, i.e., they are used as supportive roles within theology. Apologists are not going to convince intelligent historians that the historians should include supernatural components in their historical-critical methodology. For those who adhere to orthodox Christian theology, any acceptance of supernatural claims by a recipient must reside in the Spirit's conviction after reading or hearing the gospel. Scripture is either inspired, or it is not inspired; it is either the foundation of the Christian faith, or it is not. Historical inquiry certainly is not the foundation; it may be a supplement, at best. Paul attests to this in the book of Timothy: "All scripture is inspired by God and is useful for teaching, for reproofing, for correcting, and for training in righteousness" (2 Tim 3:16). Paul is not saying that Scripture is intended to normalize Christian faith in the areas of doctrine, as some unorthodox apologists have attempted to do by connecting theology to modern political and social movements, but to establish it. Paul does not begin with an established righteousness or theology and work backward by saying whatever faith you can imagine, Scripture is useful for justifying or normalizing it. Paul is placing emphasis on the importance of Scripture: it is foundational. If the Bible did not exist, where would faith originate? This work would not suffice to cover an overview even of oral tradition.

However, before continuing with the premise on Paul's remarks in the book of Timothy, it is necessary to review some concepts that were included in a previous volume related to this work. Research on this topic that resulted in the publication of *Early Christianity and Historical Methods* suggests that at least one of the Gospels (in written form) was in circulation much earlier than current scholarship has dated it. The full explanation will not be rehearsed here but only a brief summation. In 1 Corinthians, referring to Christ's atonement, Paul states "that he was buried, that he was raised on the third day in accordance with the Scriptures" (1 Cor 15:4). Paul's writings are dated around 55 CE. A proposal is made: if the Gospels were dated, at the earliest, 70 CE, why would Paul be specific, mentioning "the third day"? The Old Testament does not directly foretell that Christ will be raised on "the third day." It seems Paul would have obtained this information from one of the Gospels not yet written, supposedly. Paul does not say according to tradition, but according to the Scriptures. Thus, it is not likely that he is referencing oral tradition. Paul's previous words, "the things which I received I pass on as of first importance," do not negate the possibility of it being in writing form. Moreover, the language Paul uses in 1 Thessalonians 5:1–12 strongly resembles the language Jesus uses in Matthew 24:20–43, i.e., "thief in the night." Further, Galatians 4:4 appears to be taken directly from Matthew's birth narrative.

Most scholars from the academy refute the idea that this passage in Corinthians is pertaining to New Testament writings. They believe that Paul is referring to the Old Testament when he uses the phrase "according to the Scriptures." However, their explanation for Paul's specific language is more subjective than the direct accusation developed in *Early Christianity and Historical Methods*. They have to divide up the passage into separate categories to support their belief, i.e., in one part Paul is referencing tradition, then switches to the Old Testament. It seems that it's permissible to argue outside the context if it fits the prevailing narrative in academia.

The premise of the argument in *Early Christianity and Historical Methods* supports the context of the passage without resorting to exegetical acrobats. This discloses the subjectivity of each critic's approach to interpreting passages of the text. There is nothing that could be considered sensational or miraculous in the argument, i.e., the book of Matthew was written earlier than the prevailing consensus accepted by the academy. However, it indirectly impacts the historical narrative related to the validity of the theology. For example, if the composition of the book of Matthew was much closer to the events, it becomes more of a challenge to deny the accuracy due to the passing of time and precise recollection of events by the author. This research is generally indifferent as to whether or not the textual critique supports Christianity. In this case, however, the textual critique clearly does.

Nevertheless, back to the remarks by Paul in 2 Timothy 3:16: the word γραφή can be translated as "writing" in English. However, as many biblical language scholars have argued, "the study of the words alone will not present us with a consistent interpretation or theology."[1] If the passage is put into context, the reader will clearly understand the way in which the word is used in this passage. It is no doubt referencing the Old Testament exclusively. For example, the preceding verse states, "And how from childhood you have known the sacred writings that are able to instruct you for salvation through faith in Jesus Christ" (2 Tim 3:15). τά ἱερά γράμματα, or "sacred scriptures," signifies that the author is exclusively referring to the Old Testament. This potential fallacy falls under what D. A. Carson titles "Appeal to Unknown or Unlikely Meanings" in *Exegetical Fallacies* (nearly identical to Köstenberger and Patterson's title in fallacy 3 of their work).[2] Carson warns

---

1. Barrick, "Exegetical Fallacies," 15–27.
2. Köstenberger and Patterson, *Invitation to Biblical Interpretation*, 635.

against poor research, depending on others, and meanings that do not fit the context.³ Semantics are also important for proper exegesis. The verb mood indicates the author's portrayal or representation of certainty.⁴ For example, you "have known" the sacred writings that are able to instruct you. The only sacred writings that Timothy knew were from the Old Testament. Thus, the Greek word γραφή in this context applies exclusive to the Old Testament writings. These writings, according to orthodoxy, are inspired—God-breathed—they are the foundation of the Christian faith.

Moreover, Peter attests the writings from Paul, that now make up much of the New Testament, are also included:

> ὡς καὶ ἐν πάσαις ταῖς ἐπιστολαῖς, λαλῶν ἐν αὐταῖς περὶ τούτων· ἐν οἷς ἔστι δυσνόητά τινα, ἃ οἱ ἀμαθεῖς καὶ ἀστήρικτοι στρεβλοῦσιν, ὡς καὶ τὰς λοιπὰς γραφάς, πρὸς τὴν ἰδίαν αὐτῶν ἀπώλειαν.

> As in all the epistles, he [Paul] speaks of concerning this; in which are hard to understand, which the ignorant and unstable pervert, as also they do with the Scriptures, for their own destruction.⁵

Peter has categorized Paul's epistles with other writings, presumably those familiar to the readers—Old Testament Scripture. This suggests that Paul's writings were equally important as Scripture to those alive during the composition of them.

Those who hold these beliefs are indeed presuppositional, based on the conviction of the Spirit emanating from Scripture. Also, it would be difficult to test anything without a foundation—Scripture. Abner Chou's work *The Hermeneutics of the Biblical Writers* demonstrates that the legitimate meaning of Scripture produced by "dual authorship" is evident in revelation and inspiration, i.e., the human intent of Scripture is God's intent which is the legitimate meaning. Chou uses several passages to support his argument—2 Peter 1:21, Romans 10:16, Acts 28:25, and Galatians

---

3. Carson, *Exegetical Fallacies*, 37–38.
4. Wallace, *Greek Grammar*, 445, 449.
5. My own translation of 2 Pet 3:16.

Textual Analysis and Historical Critique

3:8. Interestingly, he also uses 2 Timothy 3:16 to argue the Bible is foundational for the faith: "The text is not a series of interpretive possibilities or the ideas of the reader but the intent of the Lord."[6] Accordingly, Chou argues that "the text is not a blank slate upon which one can impose his ideas but fixed to the author's intent."[7] He goes on to say: "Knowing God's Word is foundational for godly living."[8]

In short, both of these passages from the two separate epistles by Paul must be understood in the context that the author intended. Paul was referring to the Old Testament in the book of Timothy. In I Corinthians, however, the language used suggests Paul is referencing the Gospel of Matthew.

Considering such, again, these testimonies (pertaining to the miraculous) should not be subjected to the historical-critical method, because they are based on metaphysical qualities or supernatural claims. Further, there are different philosophical approaches used to understand the events related to the disciplines of theology and history. If the historical-critical method is used to understand events related to miraculous theological claims, the sources themselves come into question. This is especially problematic when constructing arguments that allegedly originated from eyewitnesses regarding miraculous explanations.

A popular argument among apologists is that men and women would not be willing to die for a lie. This is not a strong argument when searching for certainty. The biblical witnesses are not the problem, as the argument is sometimes made by opponents. The departure from reality is the problem, i.e., miracles.

The following are examples found in history pertaining to supernatural events and eyewitnesses. In Livy's history of Rome, dozens of Roman senators claim that Romulus was taken up to heaven in their midst (eyewitnesses). To add to the credibility of this story, a well-respected advisor, Proculus Julius, testifies that he had an encounter with Romulus after his death, explaining to

---

6. Chou, *Hermeneutics of Biblical Writers*, 28.
7. Chou, *Hermeneutics of Biblical Writers*, 28.
8. Chou, *Hermeneutics of Biblical Writers*, 13.

Ancient Literature and Philosophy of Religion

the people that it was the will of heaven that "Rome should be the capital of the world."[9] And there's the Dionysus cult (adherents to the god of wine and animal life), which flourished in the Greco-Roman world (c. 450 BCE to the fourth century of the common era). In Rome, writing in the second century BCE, Livy describes how problematic they had become. The senate took measures to curb their numbers by executing hundreds of them. However, the threat of death did not deter their religious convictions, as they continued to flourish, despite persecution reaching numbers in the thousands.[10] Perhaps their convictions caused them to believe Dionysus was not a lie, or they were willing to die for a lie. Regardless, from a historical-critical perspective, the same charge could be applied to the Christians.

The historical record suggests that many people have been willing to die for a lie. Another example is Constantine. Arguably, he used a lie to unite the Roman Empire. Christianity may be true, but some scholars have argued that Constantine did not actually believe it was true. There are, however, worse things than death for a Roman, and relinquishing control of an empire is at the top. Whether he actually believed in Christianity or not, Constantine convinced his entire army that Christianity was real. Motivating them to believe, he instructed them to paint the symbol of Christ (XP, the first two letters of Christ in Greek) on their shields before the primary battle that resulted in his sole control of the empire. Constantine's gamble paid off, not necessarily because he was a believer but because he convinced others to believe. He was not an eyewitness, but he was willing to wager his empire on what he likely thought was a lie. Moreover, he continued to have a direct impact on major aspects of the religion. The point is, many people are willing to die for a lie, because they have other motives.

What would be the motives for Christian eyewitnesses in antiquity? It's difficult to psychoanalyze an ancient mind, but that doesn't prevent scholars from trying. Michael Goulder was a scholar who taught biblical studies at the University of Birmingham. He

9. Dodson and Smith, *Exploring Biblical Backgrounds*, 217–18.
10. Metzger, *New Testament*, 84–85.

Textual Analysis and Historical Critique

appeals to psychological conditions for explaining the resurrection. Goulder argues that Peter was so overwhelmed with guilt and grief that his encounters with Jesus after his death were hallucinations rather than physical encounters. Peter shared his experiences with other followers who began to have similar experiences in groups. Goulder tries to explain why Paul converted to Christianity by claiming Paul felt restricted and in bondage to the Jewish law—Judaism—and this caused him to hallucinate.[11]

Such arguments are not accepted here, but the Christian faith should not rest on the notion that eyewitnesses would not be willing to die for a lie. The key is biblical orthodoxy, i.e., the inspiration of Scripture—the Spirit convicts its recipients and they believe. A critical approach to the history will not suffice to convince and certainly not convict those who practice the methods of studying ancient history. The passage in Matthew 28 does not commission followers to "go out and convince through argumentation" but to spread the gospel and teach converts, i.e., spread the message and God's Spirit will convict. This is the long-held orthodox view of the Christian religion. Today, it varies considerably among modern contemporaries. The intention here, however, is to provide clarity between historical and theological approaches to certain events in the past. There exist many philosophical theories on justifying religious beliefs. The next section provides a brief overview.

Faith and Reason

In book 1 of *The Nature of the Gods*, Cicero declares theology (the nature of the gods) to be the noblest of studies for the human mind to grasp.[12] He also points out (via Epicurus) that God must exist, because nature had imprinted the concept in the minds of all humanity. "For what nation or category of men does not have some anticipation of gods, without being indoctrinated?"[13]

---

11. Steele, *Early Christianity*, 56.
12. Cicero, *Nature of the Gods*, bk 1, 3.
13. Cicero, *Nature of the Gods*, bk 1, 18.

Ancient Literature and Philosophy of Religion

The goal in this section will be to analyze and discuss the relationship between faith and reason by evaluating select philosophical theories on the subject: fideism, strong rationalism, and critical rationalism.

Fideism argues a person must be committed by taking a "leap of faith" that is, believing without any evidence to show that your belief is true. They refuse to engage in any kind of reason that would substantiate their beliefs, arguing their faith is enough. If the fideist is accused of being irrational, he will point out, any argument must rest on premises or assumptions of some kind. Because they do not grant such irrational charges to their philosophical theory, this makes it difficult to argue with a fideist.[14] From the fideists' position, testing their belief system against a rational or reasonable standard would be a mistake, because faith alone is the foundation of their belief system; in doing so, the person loses faith. Kierkegaard was a strong supporter of fideism. Kierkegaard argues, "Without risk, there is no faith. Faith is precisely the contradiction between the infinite passion of the individual's inwardness and the objective uncertainty."[15]

In contrast, strong rationalism will argue before accepting a belief system that it must be possible to prove the belief is true. A strong supporter of this view is William K. Clifford. Clifford argues, "We may believe what goes beyond our experience, only when it is inferred from that experience by the assumption that what we do not know is like what we know."[16] Clifford argues that to not question one's belief system and stifle his inquiry, the life of this person, is one long sin against mankind.[17]

Critical rationalism finds fault in both the above approaches, specifically, because no system can provide a conclusive universal proof. Critical rationalism requires a person to use rational capabilities to the greatest extent possible and compare conclusions to opposing or alternative religious views. Some critical rationalists

---

14. Peterson et al., *Reason and Religious Belief*, 58–59.
15. Peterson et al., *Reason and Religious Belief*, 59.
16. Clifford, "Ethics of Belief," 309.
17. Peterson et al., *Reason and Religious Belief*, 55.

believe that to be true to their philosophy, one must develop arguments that would be acceptable by any reasonable person. Still, they understand not everyone will accept their position. Nonetheless, it is essential for being a reasonable believer in this philosophy.[18] It is possible to test religious beliefs through logic and evidence without ceasing to have faith in these beliefs, for example, to apply certain epistemological arguments, such as special revelation tied to the inspiration of Scripture, even when evidence is circumstantial, i.e., it is purely metaphysical stemming from the person's conviction. Likewise, it is possible to test religious beliefs with logic and evidence and lose faith in these beliefs, although not in the way the fideist claims. For example, if one tests a belief and finds it lacking, one may feel justified in surrendering that belief. The decision to initiate the very test itself has no consequence of putting one's faith in jeopardy—providing one applies the correct combination of epistemology. This would also apply within orthodoxy—testing beliefs with the Scriptures.

Alvin Plantinga has developed a way to test and justify beliefs called the A/C model. He takes arguments from Thomas Aquinas and John Calvin to expand and develop the model, hence the name A/C model. Plantinga analyzes warranting Christian belief through justification without evidence, i.e., if a person considers all criticism and contrary opinions but still accepts the Christian doctrine on the basis of proposition evidence, that person is justified. Plantinga provides the following example: a person considers and reflects on Nietzsche and all his claims of weak Christians, then concludes that this claim, Nietzsche's claim, does not correspond to the evidence or experience he has known throughout his life; thus, he is justified in concluding the evidence is more convincing for accepting Christian doctrine.[19] Plantinga makes it clear that such a person could be mistaken, a victim of an illusion or wishful thinking, but still justified in his beliefs.

Plantinga develops the argument further by connecting reason and faith, disclosing the teachings of Aquinas and Calvin—a

18. Peterson et al., *Reason and Religious Belief*, 62.
19. Plantinga, *Knowledge and Christian Belief*, 17–18.

natural knowledge of God and how these beliefs constitute knowledge. He contends the A/C model—natural knowledge of God—is not arrived at by quick inferences that trigger its operation. According to Plantinga, a person doesn't marvel at the night sky and conclude there must be a God. Rather, it is the perception of the night sky that causes these beliefs to just arise within us. In short, these beliefs arise as a circumstance of our encounter with certain natural grand occurrences; they are not conclusions from them.

This philosophy originates in Calvin's cognitive mechanism referred to as *"sensus divinitatis,"* that is, a sense of divinity that produces in humanity belief in God. Everyone is born with this innate element—*sensus divinitatis*—or at least has the capacity for it, which develops as the person ages; when it functions properly, it produces in us belief in God. However, when this function is compromised or weakened by sin, the sense of divinity is suppressed, enabling the person to reject the existence of God, because the evidence within the person has become so weakened. This philosophy contrasts with Karl Marx's theory that those who hold belief in God suffer from cognitive dysfunction.[20]

An element of theology related to how beliefs are tested is the ontological argument. Alvin Plantinga critiques the ontological argument. First, we will focus on his development of the argument, that is, *the Argument Triumphant*. Plantinga argues, "If a proposition is impossible in at least one possible world, then it is impossible in every possible world; what is impossible does not vary from world to world." Hence, premise 33 (there is no omnipotent, omniscient, and morally perfect being) is impossible in the actual world; rendering the existence of a being to actually exist in every possible world with these qualities.[21] Essentially, it is possible that God (maximally great being) exists. God exists out of necessity; he is not contingent on anything. Thus, God's existence is of necessity, or he does not exist. Therefore, God exists. Plantinga contends the problem with the argument is with the first premise; if it is rejected the rest of the argument doesn't hold. He goes on

---

20. Plantinga, *Knowledge and Christian Belief*, 31–35, 37.
21. Plantinga, *God, Freedom, and Evil*, 112.

Textual Analysis and Historical Critique

to say the argument does not prove God's existence, but it proves to be rational. Perhaps a person would not view this as inferring belief. Still, the belief system is not irrational, nor would a person be necessarily justified in dismissing belief.

Strong rationalism is a position held by many to avoid superstition. While empiricists believe all knowledge has its origin in experience, rationalists believe that knowledge belongs to the development and principles within the mind itself—innate ideas. Strong rationalists do not reject experience, but they believe it is insufficient for producing true knowledge.

There is some overlap between these philosophical branches, which has resulted in many apologists attempting to apply an induction theory to the resurrection of Jesus. First, it should be noted, the inductive argument, which is tied to empiricism, does have a weakness. For example, the premise in the inductive argument does not provide a logical guarantee that the conclusion is true; it attempts to establish evidence through observation that the conclusion is true. Take the example of swans. Swan 1, 2, 3 . . . 1000 are white. Therefore, all swans are white. The fact that every swan we have observed until now has been white provides good evidence for assuming the next swan we observe will be white; but it provides no guarantee that all swans are white. In fact, the next swan we observe may be black.[22] In Europe, everyone did believe all swans were white, until black swans were discovered in 1697 during the exploration of Australia.[23]

Now that the problem with induction has been addressed, a person must decide if a certain degree of reason is needed to accept the Christian faith. Indeed, many believe a certain amount of reason is required, otherwise religious beliefs could morph into superstition. The facts are: history and archaeology can and do confirm many of the events in the Bible (evidence-based). Accepting Scripture through divine revelation and submitting that Jesus Christ is the Son of God who died on the cross and was resurrected, sparing humanity from eternal damnation (supernatural/

22. Law, *Philosophy*, 180.
23. Minter, "Facts of Black Swan," para. 3.

metaphysics), cannot be proven using the same standards history and archaeology use to confirm basic historical truths. Tangible evidence is available in the historiography and archaeological records regarding Jesus as a historical figure, e.g., crucifixion and other various non-miraculous events recorded in the Bible. In short, many biblical accounts (excluding the miraculous) are compared and substantiated by archaeology and history. This is the limit to inductive reasoning: it is best utilized in conjunction with physical evidence. Evidence such as divine revelation, miracles, and Christ's resurrection cannot be established using this method. It can be inferred only via deduction considering the tangible evidence that is available.

In contrast, the opposition, using the method of induction, will insist their argument based on known reality has a higher probability of being true, rendering these miraculous and metaphysical claims false. This provides them with the justification for rejecting the metaphysical and supernatural events pertaining to the resurrection. Some of the historiography related to the events surrounding Jesus (excluding the miraculous) can be substantiated. Reiterating Clifford, "We may believe what goes beyond our experience, only when it is inferred from that experience by the assumption that what we do not know is like what we know."[24] Essentially, Clifford is saying we are allowed to believe something that goes beyond our experience only if it infers by way of what we do know or have experienced. Clifford likely would not object to rationalizing a belief, but the belief must infer a past experience to be justified. He uses the example of how scientists infer the existence of hydrogen in the sun. It would be correct to assume this approach would require extreme philosophical maneuvering for the apologist to embrace and apply it to his religion. Regardless, many apologists have used derivatives of this theory to various religious claims in history. The problem is "inferences of the historical kind are more precarious and less exact than inferences in many other sciences."[25]

24. Clifford, "Ethics of Belief," 309.
25. Clifford, "Ethics of Belief," 308.

Textual Analysis and Historical Critique

David Hume is well known for pointing out weaknesses of inductive reasoning in *A Treatise of Human Nature*. Basically, preference is given to the greatest number of past observations.[26] Hume avoids logical contradiction by using probability. It goes something like this: if the event in question has never occurred in the past, the probability of the claim is false. Probabilities, of course, are not guarantees, as previously demonstrated. Nevertheless, applying induction to miraculous and metaphysical claims provides justification for either rejecting them or deeming them inconclusive at best. The example of the swans has given reason for some to pause. However, the majority of scholars continue with their methodology as if there will never be a black swan that contradicts humanity's long-established experience with reality.

Those that do test their belief system often discover logic and reason can establish evidence of physical occurrences within the historical record (artifacts, ancient texts, etc.) but only provide inference to the metaphysical (resurrection, atonement for sin, etc.). So, while it is possible to test belief systems to an extent, there is a risk of losing one's faith, but not for the reason the fideist argues. Further, blindly accepting a belief system can be dangerous and tragic for those who are exposed to radical religious leaders. For this reason, many apologists argue that justification should be considered before accepting a belief system.

Plantinga's A/C model provides a good explanation for justifying a belief system. Specifically, as it pertains to God and why some people are able to deny God's existence (suppressed sense of divinity), while others are able to justify the belief in God through *sensus divinitatis*. The philosophical theory people use to justify their beliefs should not have an impact on their critical scholarship, although it almost always does. Apologists will consciously or unconsciously make connections favorable to their beliefs from the historical record.

Still, scholars in the academy should recognize that orthodoxy is not as easily dismissed as superstition. Theologians who adhere to a semblance of the fideist position are more capable of

---

26. L. Henderson, "Problem of Induction."

producing solid academic conclusions from the historical record, because faith alone is the foundation for their belief system. They have never relied exclusively on physical evidence to sustain their beliefs; they have managed to secure a balanced epistemology. In other words, they never argue that the historical-critical method substantiates their faith.

History and Scripture

The historical-critical method has its place within biblical studies, but it was never intended to produce or truly understand theology. To suggest that the theological is secondary to the historical is counterintuitive to orthodoxy. It denies the inspiration of Scripture by reducing the Bible to the semblance of a history book. For the orthodox theologian, the theological message embedded within the text by the divine Author is more important than the human author's accuracy. Second Corinthians 5:16 affirms that followers of Christ no longer know him according to the flesh (in physical human form) but through faith. It is the historical Jesus whom critical scholarship is concerned with knowing, not the Christ. In being so concerned, critical scholars overlook the Christ and theology communicated by the divine Author. Moreover, it is erroneous to suggest the Bible is not foundational to the faith yet to claim the probability of the resurrection positions Jesus as the foundation, as many apologists argue. In the absence of the Bible, Jesus is unknowable. There is no account of the crucifixion outside the Bible, only hearsay from a few sources such as Pliny, Tacitus, and Flavius Josephus—whom many believe to have been an opportunist.[27] Pliny reports only what he hears about the Christians from various sects within the community—some of it very disturbing.[28] Tacitus is a good source for establishing the historicity of Jesus as a man, but he states only that Jesus was condemned to death. After

---

27. Metzger, *New Testament*, 89–90.
28. Wilken, *Christians as Romans Saw*, 15–17.

Textual Analysis and Historical Critique

Josephus's death, many in the academy argue that Christian scribes artificially inserted Josephus's confession regarding Jesus's divinity.

In short, the unfolding of events recorded in the entire Bible is what establishes the foundation for Christianity. If all that existed were outside sources (like those mentioned above) for Christ's atonement and the resurrection, there would be no faith. The record would consist of a man who managed to gather a small group of follows, upset the establishment, and was sentenced to death.

Orthodox Christians rely strictly on the accounts provided by the Bible for understanding Christ and his message of salvation. The Bible is not history proper. According to orthodoxy, however, it has been inspired by God. If the Bible is removed from the foundation and Jesus's teaching alone became the foundation of the faith, that would help to bridge the gap between secularism and orthodoxy.

However, it would eliminate long-held tradition, such as the sanctity of marriage, the sanctity of life, and nearly anything seculars may view as problematic for the modern age. The mentality shifts to "sure, the Bible is profitable for instruction and . . . , but it's also antiquated." Essentially, in this view, all that is required is Jesus and his message of forgiveness. Sacred Scripture is reduced to a form of history—a history written by men of their time, no longer relevant for anyone after the Enlightenment. Profitable? Perhaps, but not inspired.

Again, in the context of Paul's attestation regarding the profitability of Scripture, it is profitable because it is inspired by God. The γραφή that Paul is referencing is the Old Testament—Scripture. The foundation of the Christian faith rests on the entire Bible and its message; this includes creation, original sin, God's redemption plan, prophecies, fulfillment, and reconciliation through Christ.

The church fathers made no distinction between what they called θεόπνευστος (God-inspired) and the canonical writings.[29] This is because they had a different criterion for including books in the canon. Athanasius, Didymus the Blind, and Rufinus composed a canonical list nearly identical to each other. Did they get

---

29. Metzger, *Canon of New Testament*, 256.

it right? Most theologians who understand the criteria they used believed they did. Here is where the historical-critical method can be applied: historians prefer sources that are closest to the time of the events. Technically, there is nothing extraordinary regarding the church fathers' methods for compiling and declaring certain books canonical. The canon was a recognition of the writings that made their authority known based on the recurring theme seen throughout the period—orthodoxy, apostolicity, and consensus among the churches. If the books in question contained two of these characteristics—orthodoxy and apostolicity—and the churches agreed they did, the books were recognized as canonical.

5

Literature and Theology

THE LITERARY WORK OF the past often means different things to various people at different times. However, the meaning in the literary work from the past, originally assigned by the author(s), remains constant. The reader often assigns significance to ancient literature that is determined by the reader's worldview. Literary critic Terry Eagleton argues that "the present is only ever understandable through the past, with which it forms a living continuity, and the past is always grasped from our own partial viewpoint within the present."[1] It should be recognized there are difficulties when readers attempt to determine the significance of ancient religious writings, i.e., produce a theological message within the work. This is because each person who is attempting to secure the meaning of the work will be influenced by his or her presuppositions, which were developed from his or her religious views—Christian, Jewish, etc. Eagleton's statement above captures most postmodern thought regarding literature. However, this is partially because these modern readers are not trained historians, bible scholars, philosophers, or theologians. Thus, they simply apply all they read through a modern perspective. This can be mostly resolved by taking appropriate steps to understand the culture and background of an author, specifically the ancient authors. Understanding how

1. Eagleton, *Literary Theory*, 62.

Ancient Literature and Philosophy of Religion

the authors made sense of their world and their cultural practices will provide a better understanding of what they meant to convey to their audience. The orthodox theologian does not take this task lightly, because the theology that emerges must be consistent throughout both texts, the Old and New Testaments.

Postmodern criticism need not influence a person's confidence or faith in Scripture regarding authority. The Bible contains textual issues, and some scholars have even made allegations of errors in the text. These accusations, however, would not extend to areas of faith or the Christian message. The errors are inadvertent errors (mostly) and not an indication of falsehood. In matters of faith and salvation, the Scriptures have preserved their spiritual truths.

The Bible can be considered authoritative without committing to the exactness a critical scholar anticipates for determining accuracy. Christians can be confident that regardless of whether or not textual criticism has unveiled a 100 percent reconstruction (in the concept of linguistic patterns, and as Craig Blomberg suggests—the impossibility of critics reaching 100 percent)[2] of the original words of the text, the authority of Scripture remains. Theologian Millard Erickson argues: God, a veracious being, will desire that humanity is not being misled by Scripture. Therefore, according to orthodox theology, the Bible is dependable and trustworthy, the authority on all things it teaches, when correctly interpreted.[3] History complements theology, and much can be learned about church history through the study of history. However, history cannot substantiate theological beliefs that contain metaphysical or spiritual components. Textual criticism may provide enough clarity regarding what the autographs contained, depending on the view of the scholar, making it feasible to construct a reliable interpretation. Nevertheless, it is the Christian's faith, i.e., what many theologians refer to as "special revelation," that attests to the spiritual message in Scripture. "These things God has revealed to us through the Spirit; for the Spirit searches everything, even the

---

2. Blomberg and Foutz, *Handbook of New Testament*, 18.
3. Erickson, *Christian Theology*, 194, 209.

Literature and Theology

depths of God" (1 Cor 2:10). The way to know God is through Scripture; the irony of this paradox is not lost.

In his work *Hermeneutics as Apprenticeship*, David Starling focuses on the process of achieving hermeneutical wisdom and lays out an apprenticeship for interpretive practices.[4] A noteworthy claim Starling makes is that Christ is central to Scripture, but without Scripture, Christ is unknowable.[5] He makes the argument that both unity and plurality of Scriptures are important. Starling also distinguishes the difference in the Old Testament covenant and the days when God's Spirit had already been poured out upon his people.[6] Starling uses 1 Corinthians as a guide for "doing theology."[7] Paul did not come to preach the gospel with wisdom and eloquence, as Starling points out. The words of Paul in this passage are a critical element within epistemology, i.e., understanding Jesus the historical figure and Jesus as the Christ: "The message of the cross is foolishness to those who are perishing" (1 Cor 1:18). Starling shows how Paul makes use of the Old Testament and warns those who wish to go beyond the Bible for theology. "Those who seek to build anything in God's church (theological systems included) should work in fear and trembling before him, resisting the delusion that they could improve on his plans and specifications by adding some flourish of their own that goes beyond what is written."[8] Starling demonstrates that the New Testament authors' use of the Old Testament and textual criticism by New Testament authors regarding Old Testament meanings are critical aspects of the hermeneutical apprenticeship. In other words, they remind the reader to approach the Bible as a whole.

The question is, how we can be confident of the New Testament authors' exegesis of the Old Testament passages? Perhaps because the variations that would have been circulating during the apostles' time would relate to orthographic style—script and

---

4. Starling, *Hermeneutics as Apprenticeship*, 20–21.
5. Starling, *Hermeneutics as Apprenticeship*, 24.
6. Starling, *Hermeneutics as Apprenticeship*, 46.
7. Starling, *Hermeneutics as Apprenticeship*, 131.
8. Starling, *Hermeneutics as Apprenticeship*, 137.

the modernization of grammar. This is evident at Qumran where scribes were practicing a type of textual criticism by placing dots above and below characters and words that indicated a variation, where a word or character was to be removed (among other practices). However, these different versions contained within the Qumran scrolls point to variants in the Hebrew tradition. The multiplicity of text types at Qumran between 300 BCE and 135 BCE resulted in a single and authoritative text by 135 BCE, at the latest. After the destruction of the temple, the Masoretic Text (MT) was the only existing text in Jewish circles; the Septuagint was no longer an influence for the Jews, because it was used by Christians. From the writing of the individual books until 300 BCE, the Old Testament was updated in terms of spelling, vowels, grammar, and script type, i.e., from archaic script to those copied and transmitted in the square script. According to some scholars, these revisions did not change the content of the Old Testament.[9]

If textual criticism was a practice among the Qumran scribes, it may be assumed that apostles who were educated (like Paul) would also have been capable of engaging in textual criticism to understand the author's original intent. An example is found in one of Paul's epistles, where either Paul was writing better than he knew for future generations of Christians (i.e., under the influence of God's inspiration) or did engage in some type of hermeneutics.[10] For example, Paul's epistle to the Philippians was instrumental regarding the Godhead for the future of the church's doctrine and defense against heresies.

One Greater Than Jonah

Some theologians worry that biblical texts are being studied as strictly historical documents, absent of revelation or theology. This can be problematic, since these texts are not history proper. The theologians argue that biblical interpretation must be grounded in

---

9. Brotzman and Tully, *Old Testament Textual Criticism*, 25–31.
10. See Steele, *Early Christianity*, 13–15.

Literature and Theology

history and cultural aspects related to language. However, the recoded historical contents within the text should not be approached as merely a human phenomenon.[11] The divinely inspired revelation that originates from Scripture is a critical part of the interpretation process, and it should take precedence over the historicity. Köstenberger and Patterson, for example, make this clear in their book, *Invitation to Biblical Interpretation:* "Thus, we have argued that history, language, and theology form a hermeneutical triad with theology at the apex."[12]

The following analysis of Jonah and Matthew considers Old and New Testament connections while keeping the theological message at the apex. These theological themes are considered from a theological worldview rather than a strictly historical. Certain critics may detect elements and patterns related to structuralism or intertextuality, i.e., both books contain passages that have a central meaning that is similar, and one book makes use of the other. According to orthodox theology, the unadulterated meaning of Scripture, as intended by the divine Author—God—can be extracted from our vantage point in history to disclose a forward-looking theological message found in the Old Testament that relates to the New Testament. For example, the theological lesson evident in the book of Jonah reveals the compassion God extended to other nations. This is a foreshadow of what is to come in the New Testament through Christ on a larger scale.

Before analyzing the theological message in the book of Jonah, it may be judicious to review the prophet's prophecy. After being thrown overboard during the storm by the sailors who were attempting to save their own lives, Jonah is swallowed by a huge fish, vomited up, and begins his journey to the great city of Nineveh. According to the text, on the first day Jonah arrives in the city, he proclaims, "Forty more days and the city will be overturned" (Jonah 3:4). Jonah does not call for the inhabitants to repent, nor does there appear to be any condition, just that the city

---

11. Köstenberger and Patterson, *Invitation to Biblical Interpretation*, 700–701.

12. Köstenberger and Patterson, *Invitation to Biblical Interpretation*, 701.

will be overturned. However, the king sets a decree and everyone, including the cattle, must repent, and they do. God shows compassion, accepts their repentance, and the city is not destroyed.

Some view this as a failed prophecy. Robert J. Miller is one who takes this position. Miller is the Rosenberger Chair of Christian and Religious Studies at Juniata College, Huntingdon, Pennsylvania. Miller argues that because Nineveh was not destroyed after forty days, Jonah was technically a false prophet, according to the criteria in Deuteronomy 18:22. Further, even if the message that God entrusted to Jonah was meant as a warning, Jonah would still be a false prophet, because the message he actually delivered was not a message of warning.[13]

Early Christians (St. Augustine, Athanasius, and St. Thomas Aquinas) attempted to show that Jonah's message was not contradictory regarding the events. They used hermeneutics to argue there was a double meaning in the Hebrew verb "overturn," "return," or "be converted." Hence, the prophecy which Jonah prophesied did come true, the city was converted. However, this manipulation of the linguistics does not change the clear fact in the narrative that God did not send his prophet to the city to warn them of their coming conversion but to threaten them.[14]

To understand a theological theme regarding the prophecy, which was minimal—"Forty more days and the city will be overturned"—deconstruction of the ancient literature must be avoided and the focus be on the prophet himself. Most of the book consists of the trials and tribulations that Jonah experienced because of his refusal to obey God and deliver the message to Nineveh.[15] The reader does not need to apply exegesis, hermeneutics, or any other linguistic applications to recognize the clear theological theme; it is a story of redemption found throughout the Old Testament. Man disobeys God (Jonah refuses to deliver message to Nineveh), he suffers the consequences (gets caught in a violent storm, is thrown overboard and swallowed by a fish), repents and returns to the right

13. Miller, *Helping Jesus Fulfill Prophecy*, 24.
14. Faj, "Stoic Features," 35–36.
15. Elata-Alster and Salmon, "Deconstruction of Genre," 41.

path (cries out to God from the belly of the fish, is spit out on land, and goes to Nineveh to deliver message from God). Jonah makes this known though his own words to God: "I knew that you are a gracious and compassionate God, slow to anger and abounding in love, a God who relents from sending calamity" (Jonah 4:2). God proved this by extending grace to the city when he saw they were remorseful; an entire city was redeemed by God's extended grace.

Perspectives

Many scholars note the book of Jonah for its inclusion of a nation outside of Israel. While Christians look to integrate it with theological facets in the New Testament, others view it as a legend, myth, or parable that conveys an artistic expression of the human experience.[16] It all depends on the readers' presuppositions likely developed though their religious affiliations. For example, while Christians view Jonah as having had a limited nationalistic view regarding God and his providence over the nation of Israel alone, the Midrash attributes Jonah's reluctance to deliver the message to his concern of becoming a false prophet. Jonah knows the city will repent and be spared, resulting in a false prophecy.[17] Nevertheless, if the cause of Jonah's disobedience is bracketed, and attention is focused on the predominate narrative, a clear theological message emerges from the text. The theological message is evident to many, regardless of presuppositions or religious affiliation: God has extended his grace to other nations outside of Israel.

David Randall Scott is a scholar associated with the Church of Jesus Christ of Latter-day Saints. In his article "The Book of Jonah: Foreshadowings of Jesus as the Christ," Scott argues there are many parallels between Jonah and Jesus. He begins with the name Jonah, which in Hebrew means "dove." The dove is a symbol of peace and is used to signal the end of the flood for Noah. It was also used as a sacrifice at the temple and represents the Holy Spirit

---

16. Pelli, "Literary Art of Jonah," 18.
17. Pelli, "Literary Art of Jonah," 22.

when it descends on Jesus after his baptism. According to Scott, all of these images point to Jesus's attributes, sacrifice, and divinity. Furthermore, Scott notes that Latter-day Saints view all prophets as a type of Christ.[18] It should be obvious, but the next section will disclose that Jonah was no Christ.

Connecting Genres of Old and New Testaments

Two separate incidents are found in the book of Jonah that disclose non-Israelites attempting to interact with the Hebrew God. The first interaction is evident among the sailors aboard the ship during the storm. In their fear and desperation, they cry out to God, asking him to spare their lives, before throwing Jonah overboard. This demonstrates the sailors' conviction that Jonah's God was the true God, the ultimate Creator and Judge.[19] The second interaction is when the Ninevites believe the message Jonah proclaims is from God. Thus, they turn from their wickedness, hoping that God will spare them. Indeed, after God sees what they do, he has compassion and does not destroy the city.[20] Are these events in the book of Jonah foreshadowings of God's future intentions regarding the inclusion of gentiles into his new covenant proclaimed in the New Testament? Although critics have doubts, many theologians believe they are. For example, the New Testament author of Matthew could have been making use of this Old Testament passage to write a narrative that would connect the new theology to the Old Testament.

The sign of the prophet Jonah, which Jesus mentions in Matthew 12:39, is the only sign this generation would receive. This is an analogy, a sign, made clear by Jesus's own words. The authors of "The Interpretation of Matthew 12:39, 40" argue that Jonah and Jesus both preach a message of repentance to the people of their time.[21] This is not exactly correct. Jonah proclaims a mes-

---

18. Scott, "Book of Jonah," 161–62.
19. Timmer, "Jonah's Theology of Nations," 20.
20. Timmer, "Jonah's Theology of Nations," 17.
21. Barnes et al., "Interpretation of Matthew 12:39, 40," 420.

Literature and Theology

sage from God to the Ninevites, just as Jesus proclaims a message from God to the people of his time; but Jesus makes it clear what is now here is greater than Jonah. Further, Jonah does not preach repentance to the city of Nineveh; he simply proclaims the city will be overturned in forty days. The king and residents of the city take it upon themselves to repent. It is absurd to connect Jonah with the redemptive story of humanity made possible by Jesus. Jonah is clearly no messiah; he is a messenger who first needs to be redeemed himself, most theologians agree.

The book of Jonah is a remarkable story that reveals the conversion and preservation of an entire city made possible by the extension of God's grace. Debates among scholars continue regarding whether or not the story represents recorded history. Some scholars date the book between 450 and 300 BCE based on language, style, and theology. This time frame is out of range of the prophet's life, as understood in 2 Kings 14:25, during the reign of King Jeroboam, around 788 BCE.[22] Nevertheless, for many orthodox theologians, the theological message contained in the book is more important than quarrelling over dates and the historicity of the story. Clearly, the sign of Jonah was a reflection of what was to come, i.e., the Son of Man being in the tomb and resurrected on the third day as Jonah was in the belly of a huge fish for three days, nothing more (Jonah himself lacked redeeming power). The theological theme in both cases is the extension of God's compassion and grace to other nations. Moreover, the vessel responsible for the action in the Old Testament (Jonah) is not the same as the one in the New Testament (Jesus Christ). God sends the prophet Jonah, who was at first stubborn and disobedient, to a people other than the Israelites to deliver a message that results in their redemption; God spares the city because of their remorseful actions. God sends his Son, the Christ, whose will was agreeable with God's, to atone for the world's sins that it might be spared through his actions. Regardless of the reader's presuppositions or religious affiliation, it is difficult to deny the fact that God, according to the book of Jonah, reaches out to a nation outside his chosen people. From

22. Zakovitch, "Jonah: Authorship and Date," 1319.

the perspective of theology, the book of Jonah reflects the future sentiments of God regarding his extended grace to other nations. Indeed, this theological message in the book of Jonah, according to orthodoxy, is a prelude or foreshadowing of the events in the New Testament; it materializes through the atonement of Christ extending salvation to people of all nations.

Western Morality

This analysis of Old Testament literature (thus far) has consisted of theological motifs and genres relatively compatible with Western morality. However, as mentioned in the introduction, this exposition seeks to present a balanced approach. To ignore the biblical literature that appears to contrast with the morality of Western society would result in a delinquent and insufficient analysis. Biblical literature that seems to disagree with Western morality is specifically relevant since many Westerners have adopted the Bible as the foundation for their morality. Questioning certain Old Testament narratives regarding genocide is not a new charge. For example, an early author on Western principles wrote extensively on the subject. Thomas Paine, one of the most influential writers on revolution and Enlightenment, believed that individual liberty could be obtained only by a mind free from "irrational beliefs inculcated by revealed religion."[23] Paine allocated a considerable amount to Scriptural exegesis in a critique of organized religion in his popular work *The Age of Reason*. He made some important critical observations regarding Scripture that would carry into contemporary society, and some of the same arguments are used by critics of religion today. The focus here will be on those critiques.

Three major religious organizations (Judaism, Christianity, Islam) have established themselves by claiming to be on a special mission ordained by God or to have a special revelation from God, or both. Each of these religions accuses the other of having the wrong belief. Moses, for example, receives a revelation from God

---

23. Paine, *Age of Reason*, xii.

Literature and Theology

in the form of tablets revealing commandments that should be followed. Paine notes that these laws contained moral precepts that a qualified legislator could produce without divine intervention. Further, these laws supposedly came directly from God to Moses. Thus the children of Israel had no obligation to believe Moses, because it would have been hearsay; God did not speak directly to them.[24] The same is applicable to the Koran. It was written in heaven and brought to Mohamad via an angel (hearsay). The Christians claim the word of God comes through divine inspiration. The foundation of Christianity, however, is from the testimony of eyewitnesses. Paine does not simply argue that because he was not there to witness such events for himself, he is justified in not accepting them. Rather, he argues that such extradentary claims must have stronger evidence for accepting or denying ("I have the right to believe them or not").[25] Neither Joseph nor Mary wrote on such events; they were reported by others—hearsay. A semblance of the same criteria occurs in the resurrection narrative where, according to critical scholars, the original authors are unknown and several decades pass before the event is recorded in writing. Nevertheless, the stories from the Old Testament are perhaps the most disturbing from a moral position.

Paine examines the Old Testament and considers the atrocities committed by the Israelites at God's command. He then questions if the Creator of humanity would actually commission such acts.[26] For example, Deuteronomy 7:2, Joshua 11:12, Joshua 10:40, 1 Samuel 15:3, and others suggest brutal warfare tactics. This worldview, though not entirely unjustified, is influenced by the Enlightenment faith—believing that humanity could be perfected if the correct social system is prescribed. Unfortunately, a social system of this caliber is impossible to achieve without eliminating personal freedoms and individualism, e.g., the recipients of such policies have historically been inflicted with severe oppression by tyrannical rulers. Here is where the apologist typically attempts to

24. Paine, *Age of Reason*, 7.
25. Paine, *Age of Reason*, 7.
26. Paine, *Age of Reason*, 84.

offer some sort of comforting answer to the reader, to help ease any discomfort regarding immoral action prescribed by God. Safe spaces may be popular among institutions for younger generations of the modern era, but here we must face uncertainty and discomfort head on. Thus, the reader may be disappointed to learn there are no good answers to this issue—not in the sense that would satisfy the contemporary reader.

One thing is certain: war remains as barbaric in the modern age as it was in its infancy. Some scholars, however, argue that the modern understanding of war should not be compared to the ancient practices of war, i.e., in terms of what actions would be judged good or evil.[27] John Walton argues that "the Bible was not written in order to transfer ancient thought to resemble modern thought, and neither was it written to simply affirm the values and ideas of the ancient cognitive environment and stamp them with divine authority for all time."[28]

The first part of Walton's statement is commendable, i.e., we must understand the context in which ancient literature was written, not through a modern lens. The second part of the statement, however, requires some thought. At first, it seems to fringe on a type of philosophical relativism. Theologically, whatever God has commissioned in the past should stand through all time, unless it was explicitly recommissioned and recorded in a new covenant. Otherwise, much of orthodoxy would be reduced to a house of cards resting on the culture relativism of the time. This, however, is not what Walton appears to be advocating. "The Old Testament's legal wisdom literature in context is indeed supposed to shape Israelite society, but it is not supposed to provide a set of instructions by which anyone in any place or time can construct God's idea society."[29] This is compatible with orthodoxy, i.e., the law was not abolished but was fulfilled and recommissioned in a new covenant as indicated in the New Testament (Matt 5:17). Moreover, some argue the Old Testament's laws were not to be understood as jurisprudence. Rather, they

27. Walton and Walton, *Lost World*, 10–11.
28. Walton and Walton, *Lost World*, 10.
29. Walton and Walton, *Lost World*, 101.

Literature and Theology

were instructive, i.e., listing customs and practices meant for ancient Israel. Walton connects concepts of the conquest with concepts of the New Testament. He argues the conquest was a similar concept advocated by New Testament authors—to remove sinful attributes from one's life, not to destroy oneself.[30]

It's one thing to evaluate the past and conclude certain actions were wrong; progress is made through these types of studies in human affairs. It is counterintuitive to claim certain actions were morally wrong if they were commissioned by God. How could God act immorally? If scholars believe that these war atrocities recorded in the Bible were in fact human endeavors stamped (by humans) with divine command, they have removed any chance of inspiration supposedly contained in sacred Scripture. Our first priority is not with how the ancients practiced war; we are concerned with whether or not God commissioned such acts. Once this is established, we will examine the practices of ancient warfare. Biblical scholars may dismiss such events in the Old Testament as strictly human affairs, but this will not suffice theologically. There is no denying that the ancients had cultural practices and priorities very different from moderns. From our vantage point in time, we analyze the actions taken by historical figures with the understanding that the figures themselves were bound by their moment in time. Theologically, an eternal deity would not be bound by such constraints.

In the ancient Near East, the concept of a deity granting a king's desire was accepted as common practice. There are certain instances where this occurs in the Old Testament. However, Walton argues this idea was not prominent in Israelite thought and is completely absent in the conquest of Canaan.[31] Therefore, theologians are provided with grounds for arguing the conquest of Canaan was the desire of God, not a human endeavor. Nevertheless, they now must show that these actions recorded in the Old Testament are compatible with morality, bearing in mind that cultural relativism is a philosophical abomination and any action, whether evil or

---

30. Walton and Walton, *Lost World*, 240–42.
31. Walton and Walton, *Lost World*, 210–11.

Ancient Literature and Philosophy of Religion

good, remains constant in any era. The challenge will be to show why certain divine commands in the Old Testament pertaining to conquest were not evil, though they sometimes included killing noncombatants. In their book *The Lost World of the Israelite Conquest*, Walton and Walton argue, on linguistic grounds, that the commission to utterly destroy, as translated in English, is not the best meaning of the Hebrew word used. Rather, they believe the Hebrew word *herem* refers to the removal of something.[32] Moreover, they argue that Scripture should be understood separately from its status as ancient literature. Scripture, they argue, was not intended to provide us with moral knowledge.[33] Perhaps their argument can be considered cautionary regarding contemporary notions of violence in the name of God.

Paul Copan and Matthew Flannagan take a different approach in *Did God Really Command Genocide?* Attempting to provide comfort to the reader regarding these shocking episodes in Old Testament narratives regarding war and conquest, they argue there were several authors of the Bible. There are many human authors who composed various books of the Bible and one divine Author who assumed responsibility for the inspired message within the literature. Copan and Matthew attempt to construct a philosophical argument through a serious of philosophical premises that spare God from commissioning what many moderns view as immoral acts pertaining to war and conquest. It will not be exhaustive here, but essentially the argument is as follows. The Bible is inspired but only the parts that can be conformed to a contemporary view of morality. The disturbing passages dealing with war and conquest where the killing of innocent noncombatants was encouraged are strictly the sentiments of a human author.[34] There are a few interesting proposals, but their work is mostly an apology. Typically, apologies consist of characteristics that can be described only as conjecture, special pleading, and illusionary exegetical statements of grandeur. For example, they

---

32. Walton and Walton, *Lost World*, 170, 240.
33. Walton and Walton, *Lost World*, 100.
34. Copan and Flannagan, *Did God Really Command*, 19–22.

claim: "It would be silly to say that whatever the human author says or affirms is identical to what God says or affirms."[35] For the theologian, this may have serious theological implications: God's word was distorted—forced to the will of human authors. They continue with nonrelevant examples, overstating the obvious, and enlist the writings of renowned Christian philosopher William Lane Craig to help redefine the orthodox definition of inspiration when it comes to the Bible. Essentially, they argue that there are certain passages where the human author inserted his own emotions and beliefs into the passages, free from divine interference. Therefore, anything that contrasts with contemporary moral ideology can be blamed on the human author, and God is spared from endorsing anything moderns consider immoral.

The obvious problem is to distinguish between the divine and the human wishes in the text. In the New Testament, Paul makes the distinction clear with statements such as "I say, not the Lord." For many, clarity is equally established in the Old Testament with phrases such as "God commanded." However, if the prescribed argument of Copan and Flannagan is followed, statements in the Old Testament such as "God commanded" must be attributed to chicanery on the part of the human author. God didn't actually command it; the human authors desired it, and they have attempted to pass it off as God's desire. Copan and Flannagan attempt to remedy the dilemma by differentiating the two authors of the text (God and human) with assigned phrases (occasional and general commands) and their constructed context criteria that they admit can be complex but apparently necessary.[36] Nevertheless, their argument has merit regarding warfare and the issue with utterly destroying an enemy as an occasional command.

Copan and Flannagan also offer some interesting propositions regarding the innocent, ancient approaches to state and religion, assimilation, and crime and repentance within a nation. Theologians may find fault with certain components of their philosophy as demonstrated, but they allude to sound concepts

---

35. Copan and Flannagan, *Did God Really Command*, 20.
36. Copan and Flannagan, *Did God Really Command*, 54–58.

Ancient Literature and Philosophy of Religion

regarding genocide and warfare. Two key components of the argument emerge. First, phrases such as "he left no survivor" are extensive hyperbole in the book of Joshua.[37] Second, God's command to utterly destroy the inhabitants of the area is an extension of a crucial element in the theory of war.

For example, Carl von Clausewitz, whose theory on war continues to be studied by war strategists today, wrote extensively on this topic. Clausewitz's goal was to explain war as a universal phenomenon. His theory on war involved universal principles that could apply to war itself. In this sense, the theory holds true regarding past and future warfare. In book 8, chapter 2 of *On War*, Clausewitz states, "The overthrow of the enemy is the natural end of the act of war; and if we would keep within the strictly philosophical limits of the idea, there can be no other in reality."[38] These ideas apply to ancient warfare as well. For instance, an important concept from Clausewitz's theories is the idea of "absolute war." Clausewitz insists that a war with no limits, absolute war, is the only war in which armies should engage and that limited war should be limited only by nature, not by choice.[39]

The following brief explanation regarding Clausewitz's theory may be prudent for understanding its connection with ancient warfare. Clausewitz's theory on absolute war does not necessarily call for total destruction (although this would not be ruled out). Rather, his theory calls for joint action within a nation engaged in war. Cooperation is critical between the populous and state officials, thereby not placing limits on those charged with conducting war—the generals. Nevertheless, what the Israelites practice during the conquest is a semblance of what Clausewitz develops in his time, evident in his statements: "War therefore is an act of violence intended to compel our opponent to fulfill our will."[40] There is nothing substantial in the historiography that would suggest Clausewitz was influenced by these events in the Old Testament;

37. Copan and Flannagan, *Did God Really Command*, 84–85.
38. Clausewitz, *On War*, 666.
39. Steele, *Philosophy of War*, 5–6.
40. Clausewitz, *On War*, 3.

he was a Lutheran. Further, his primary intellectual thought was forged by his own individual experiences, and he insists that war should be a composite of a trinity with three dominate tendencies: violence and passion, uncertainty and chance, and political purpose.[41] Of the three tendencies mentioned above, violence and passion relate to the passages in question regarding Old Testament warfare. For example, Clausewitz argues, "War is in no way changed or modified through the progression of civilization.... War is an act of violence pushed to its utmost bounds."[42] Historian Peter Paret records Clausewitz's theory on absolute war as "A clash of forces freely operating and obedient to no law but their own, eventually reaches the extreme—absolute war, that is, absolute violence ending in the total destruction of one side by the other."[43]

In short, war, regardless of the era, is a terrible pursuit, which on occasion is warranted. Ideally, those who contemplate initiating war will have reservations and use every possible avenue to avoid it. However, once it becomes unavoidable, total war, as prescribes by Clausewitz, will provide the highest possible chance for securing a favorable outcome. Old Testament scholar Joe Sprinkle, whose work Copan and Flannagan enlisted to distinguish genocide from ethnic cleansing, seems to recognize some benefits of conducting a campaign of total war, i.e., Sprinkle suggests that conducting a war of utter destruction (Israelite's version of total war) would have forced Canaanite populations to retreat and live as refugees outside the region.[44] Theologians, however, must object to exegetical constructions attempting to protect God from what contemporary societies view as immoral, even evil. God indeed gives the command to utterly destroy Israel's adversaries or remove them from the area with violence—if the Waltons' definition of the Hebrew word *herem* is accepted. Of course, whether or not a deity is actually commanding a conquest is not the historian's concern.

41. See Paret, "Clausewitz."
42. Clausewitz, *On War*, bk 1, ch. 1, p. 5.
43. Paret, "Clausewitz," 199.
44. Copan and Flannagan, *Did God Really Command*, 82.

Ancient Literature and Philosophy of Religion

The theologian, however, must acknowledge it is indeed God who commands the conquest against Israel's enemy. Otherwise, the foundation for the belief system (sacred Scripture) is severely damaged, i.e., the Bible is not inspired. In this case, it is strictly a human production upon which each can impose one's own will and morality, thereby conforming it to contemporary standards. The theologian should also know that the virtual principles of warfare (similar to certain laws in physics that were present but unrealized by the ancients) existed long before anyone, including Clausewitz, recognized and recorded them. Perhaps some will be consoled by the idea that God—the Creator of all things—acts intentionally (supports a campaign of total war or utter destruction to prevent genocide) when he commissions such acts. For others, no doubt, the passages where God commands such violence will continue to be enigmatic and troubling.

Nevertheless, scholars persistently argue for context, as they should. Contextualizing warfare as a whole, i.e., putting war into its greater context, ancient warfare was no more horrific or immoral than some of the campaigns that took place in the twentieth century when the industrialized war complex reached its zenith. The use of automatic weapons in the trenches of WWI and the catastrophic events of Hiroshima and Nagasaki in WWII provide us with examples where modern industrialized nations have produced the most efficient ways to extinguish human life—although some of these events (the devastation inflicted on the two Japanese cities), it is argued, were justified because they spared more lives in the end had the decision not been made to implement them. No serious strategist objects to how the U.S. chose to end the war with Japan. For example, they do not condemn the U.S. state department for failing to call its Japanese counterparts, urging them to remove all noncombatants (women and children) from those cities because they were about to unleash total destruction in those areas. It may be difficult to find justification for the conquest, but when the event is put into proper perspective, it assumes the expectations of war in general. War, as Clausewitz argues, "is no

Literature and Theology

pastime; no mere passion for venturing and winning: no work of a free enthusiasm; it is a serious means for a serious objective."[45]

Conclusion

Considering the vast amount of time between the composition of the Old Testament, the transmission process, the closing of the Old Testament canon, and the Proto-Mesocratic preservation of the text (by hand) until the invention of the printing press in the modern era, it is remarkable such an accurate text of the Old Testament has survived. There are certain features in the Ugaritic literature that not only assist in clarifying but provide confidence in the accuracy of the Old Testament. However, the many variations existing in the historiography of the Hebrew text has proven to be the primary source for determining clarification and accuracy. The Hebrew text, therefore, has the capacity to provide clarification without the assistance of outside sources regarding textual criticism—the foundation for hermeneutical and exegetical practices.

Consider the examples provided in this study: dissimilarities between Near Eastern religious characteristics and the theological distinctions found throughout the Hebrew text regarding monotheism, omnipotence, transcendence, and the image of God reflected in humanity; insufficient linguistic and exegetical arguments attempting to connect a Canaanite hymn with Psalm 29; dissimilarities between theology and culture—what counted as righteousness—thereby identifying Ezekiel's Daniel as the same Daniel in the book of Daniel as opposed to the Daniel in the Ugaritic text; comparative methods regarding dead or scarcely used words in the book of Amos; and transmission issues such as word crowding. All of these examples demonstrate how other Near Eastern texts should be utilized in comparison.

In short, the Ugaritic literature should be considered a secondary source for supporting the Hebrew text. The similarities between the Ugaritic and Hebrew texts cannot be viewed as

---

45. Clausewitz, *On War*, bk 1.

Ancient Literature and Philosophy of Religion

one culture simply copying another regarding stories and gods. Scholars have produced too many alternative credible explanations. There are, perhaps, polemical elements in some parallels, and actual borrowing may have occurred in older Near Eastern narratives. However, the most damaging case against the majority of composite or plagiaristic claims is the fact that the historical record has revealed that the god(s) and stories contained in Ugaritic literature and those in the Old Testament are the consequences of a parallel phenomenon among two distinct and independent civilizations exhibiting cognitive similarities that in turn have produced similar cultural features.

In the most generalized terms of Christian theology, the message of the entire Bible is God's plan of redemption for humanity—how to be reconciled with God for eternity through Christ. This is the theological message from a single divine Author—God. Human authors were used to relay God's message, originating from their oral traditions that at some point began to be recorded in written form. Nevertheless, this is accepted by theologians as the inspired divine message communicated to humanity.

The historical-critical approach to the Bible is much different. Its primary concern is not with the theology—apart from cultural beliefs that may have influenced the human authors. The primary concern of the historical critic is to evaluate the historicity of the literature—dates, authorship, external influences, etc. This approach is not concerned with spiritual claims or whether or not there is a message from God embedded within the literature. The critical historian will never conflate the history with theology. There is no possible way (from this critical approach) to show any probability that providence had a role in human history. Then again, there is no possible way to show providence was absent in history. Modern historians do not accept a miraculous explanation for past events. Moreover, if people can reason themselves into something, they can reason themselves out of it, just as easily. History and philosophy have a limited role in theology.

Advancing the argument, either Scripture contains inspiration where the Spirit can convict the reader or it is simply an exaggerated history book that must convince the reader. Historians never argue that if there is no practical explanation to account for the probability of an event, it must have been divine intervention.

In contrast, it is the theologian's duty to understand history in terms of a divine plan for humanity. To act otherwise is antithetical to the discipline's purpose. Therefore, like the critical historian, the theologian must approach history with certain presuppositions. This does not mean that all theological developments lack critical scholarship. To the contrary, theologians must determine what the human authors wrote from the original text before they can exegete any theological meaning. Thus, the passages must also be understood in context, which requires a comprehensive understanding of culture and background. Historical methods and philosophical reasoning play a role in the overall process. Grant Osborne was correct: "The theologian is asked to be an expert exegete, historian, and philosopher."[46]

If theologians surrender and accept abstract claims refuting providential narratives, they jeopardize the value and relevance of the discipline they practice. Curiously, in the modern era, there is often no real difference between secular scholars and many contemporary Christian theologians. For example, both argue for identical social and political objectives for humanity. Thus the question is proposed: why not join the moral philosophers? Essentially, they offer the same thing without the stigma of religion. If theologians are to remain relevant, they must use their given skills and courage to defend their position from what has been the foundation of their faith—the sacred Scriptures. That's a monumental project to take on, and the theologian will have to work much harder than the secular critic because much ground has already been relinquished.

The contention that the resurrection should not be imposed on others as a historical event is compatible with the above concern—even when holding both positions. For example, the historical-critical method can be applied to certain elements of biblical studies (textual criticism) but not to supernatural claims

---

46. Osborne, *Hermeneutical Spiral*, 384.

for validation. Was Jesus resurrected? The theologian believes Jesus was the Christ and he was resurrected. This is not a fact in the sense that it can be proven or even convincing with non-numerical probabilities—high or low—critical scholars agree. Regardless, unlike the theologian, the historian is not equipped to analyze theological claims.

The theologian must be careful not to damage the theological narrative; history will support theology, but it cannot verify it. This is why orthodox theologians, rightly so, do not capitulate to accusations such as liberties with which ancient biblical authors are charged when they composed the texts. Nor do orthodox theologians accept the argument that the Old Testament authors plagiarized, using material from other Near Eastern cultures to form their narratives. Moreover, if theologians consider prescriptive biblical passages pertaining to societal norms and virtuous living to be antiquated, they can simply apply the liberties contention to elements of the passage that are not compatible with modern society. And, as suggested, theology merges with secular moral philosophy, resulting in little if any distinction. In cases where contemporary theologians have embraced this mostly secular ideology, it has diminished their most treasured beliefs, often associated with family values.

There certainly are variations within the manuscripts of the NT, MT, LXX, and SP early on.[47] Some scholars (evangelicals) argue that what we have now mostly reflects what the original human authors wrote at the time. This study has not addressed such ambitious claims. Still, there is a uniqueness of the Old Testament's literature, and the moral standards that the theology has produced have been preserved and continued with the New Testament. Perhaps more significant for the Christian is that the theological message regarding salvation from the divine Author is constant and remains accessible. Orthodox theologians may not always be correct in their prognosis of society's condition, but they have a duty to speak truthfully about morality and God—to think about and discuss what matters most: reverence for God, virtue,

---

47. Brotzman and Tully, *Old Testament Textual Criticism*, 30–31.

nobility, family, sanctity of life, etc. The three organized Christian institutions mentioned in this study—Roman Catholic, Greek Orthodox, and Protestant—will always have disagreements. Some claim that is inevitable among those with good intentions; others point out the road to hell is also paved with good intentions. Still others will argue the tension that divides these three denominations is competition—the competition for winning souls. The challenge for many is understanding the motive behind these competitive institutions. In the modern era, souls are connected with bodies that typically have acquired voting rights and bank accounts. Theologians will have to decide to what extent they wish to be associated with these institutions.

The core principles of orthodoxy as defined here should never concede to the secular rhetoric of any age. The historian, in our modern age, is increasingly being viewed as less valuable for producing narratives on how things gradually came to be. Social scientists have taken the historians' place. Theologians will increasingly become obsolete as revisionists and deconstructionists continue to have more influence within the institutions. The ancient authors of Scripture sought to record their relationship with God, his creation, and his relationship with humanity. The same powerful institutions and social movements that have decimated the historical process have turned toward the West's most trusted and sacred text. The Bible, as it relates to Christianity, is now viewed by many not only as antiquated or outdated but as an offensive recorded version of the historiography as it relates to humanity and God. This is disappointing even for those who are not religious but study the ancient texts for insight into the evolution of human thinking and how these ancient worldviews continue to influence our thought process today—whether we realize it or not.

For many Christians, the theology that emerges from the Bible is experiential, i.e., practiced in daily life. It is capable of connecting with the deepest unconscious roots of the human psyche to engage with the individual's deep-seated emotions, producing personal convictions. On many occasions throughout history, religion was,

Ancient Literature and Philosophy of Religion

as Terry Eagleton described it for the Victorian era, "an excellent social cement" that relates to every class structure of a society.[48]

Scholars on all sides of the prism rarely approach the West's most sacred texts on its own terms. Most are restricted to a consensus deemed suitable by stale academics deeply rooted in the academy, egalitarian movements, or fundamentally influenced religious creeds developed early within the institutions. Whatever facet scholars peer through, there will be occasions where textual analysis, historical-cultural evidence, and comparative research will support theological beliefs held by religious scholars. Likewise, there will be occasions where these same principles are used to understand ancient literature but yield contradictions pertaining to certain practices and beliefs developed by organized religious institutions.

The final point in closing is this: considering the events that helped usher in history, the discovery of writing is perhaps the most significant. It not only assisted with communication and organizing society, it provided an avenue that modern scholars could utilize for accessing the ancient world. The accuracy of interpretations will be influenced by each scholar's worldview. The orthodoxy that emerges from both texts (Old and New Testaments) has a major impact on humanity. These beliefs and traditions were established early in human history. They continue to influence ideology and philosophical issues of the modern era. They have the power to unite or divide, depending on the sects' organized beliefs established by their institutions. The genesis of the civilizations analyzed in this work all share commonalities. Most notably, they developed a unity within their own community through their shared theological beliefs and myths. In our modern institutions, only an ersatz version of their tradition continues today, but access to their practices and beliefs was made possible through the recording and preservation of their sacred texts.

---

48. Eagleton, *Literary Theory*, 20.

Appendix

West Semitic Script

1700 BCE	Pro-Canaanite
1000	Phoenician
950	Palo-Hebrew Aramaic
850	Greek
600	Latin
300	Jewish (square) Nabatean
200	Samaritan
600 CE	Arabic

Bibliography

Alter, Robert. *The Writings*. Vol. 3 of *The Hebrew Bible: A Translation with Commentary*. New York: Norton & Co., 2019.
Arnold, Bill T. *Introduction to the New Testament*. New York: Cambridge University Press, 2014.
———, and Brent A. Strawn. *The World around the Old Testament: The People and Places of the Ancient Near East*. Grand Rapids: Baker Academic, 2016.
Bahn, Paul. *The Complete Illustrated History of World Archaeology*. London: Lorenz Books, 2013.
Barnes, Lemuel C., et al. "The Interpretation of Matthew 12:39, 40: A Symposium." *Biblical World* 5, no. 6 (June 1895) 417–30. https://www.jstor.org/stable/3135497.
Barrick, William D. "Exegetical Fallacies: Common Interpretive Mistakes Every Student Must Avoid." *Master's Seminary Journal* 19, no. 1 (Spring 2008) 15–27.
Beasley-Murray, G. R. "The Interpretation of Daniel 7." *Catholic Biblical Quarterly* 45, no. 1 (Jan. 1983) 44–58. https://www.jstor.org/stable/43716342.
Blomberg, Craig L., with Jennifer Foutz. *A Handbook of New Testament Exegesis*. Grand Rapids: Baker Academic, 2010.
Breisach, Ernst. *Historiography: Ancient, Medieval, and Modern*. 3rd ed. Chicago: University of Chicago Press, 2007.
Bresnan, Patrick S. *Awakening: An Introduction to the History of Eastern Thought*. 4th ed. Upper Saddle River, NJ: Prentice Hall, 2010.
Brotzman, Ellis R., and Eric J. Tully. *Old Testament Textual Criticism: A Practical Introduction*. 2nd ed. Grand Rapids: Baker Academic, 2016.
Brown, Francis, et al. *The Brown-Driver-Briggs Hebrew and English Lexicon*. Peabody, MA: Hendrickson, 2018.
Brundage, Anthony. *Going to the Sources: A Guide to Historical Research and Writing*. 5th ed. Malden, MA: John Wiley and Sons, 2013.

Bibliography

Carson, D. A. *Exegetical Fallacies*. 2nd ed. Grand Rapids: Baker Academic, 1996.

Chou, Abner. *The Hermeneutics of the Biblical Writers: Learning to Interpret Scripture from the Prophets and Apostles*. Grand Rapids: Kregel, 2018.

Cicero. *Nature of the Gods*. Translated by P. G. Walsh. New York: Oxford University Press, 2008.

Clausewitz, Carl von. *On War*. Translated by J. J. Graham. New York: Barnes & Noble, 2004.

Clifford, W. K. "The Ethics of Belief." *Contemporary Review 1866–1900* 29 (Jan. 1877) 289–309. https://www.proquest.com/docview/6659204/fulltextPDF/721D999384294E36PQ/1?accountid=12085.

Coogan, Michael D. *The Old Testament: A Very Short Introduction*. New York: Oxford University Press, 2008.

———, and Mark S. Smith. *Stories from Ancient Canaan*. 2nd ed. Louisville, KY: Westminster John Knox, 2012.

Copan, Paul, and Matthew Flannagan. *Did God Really Command Genocide? Coming to Terms with the Justice of God*. Grand Rapids: Baker, 2014.

Currid, John D. *Against the Gods: The Polemical Theology of the Old Testament*. Wheaton, IL: Crossway, 2013.

Damrosch, David, and David L. Pike, eds. *The Longman Anthology of World Literature: The Ancient World*. 2nd ed. New York: Pearson Education, 2009.

Day, John. "The Daniel of Ugarit and Ezekiel and the Hero of the Book of Daniel." *Vetus Testamentum* 30, no. 2 (Jan. 1980) 174–84. https://doi.org/10.2307/1517522.

Dodson, Derek S., and Katherine E. Smith. *Exploring Biblical Backgrounds: A Reader in Historical and Literary Contexts*. Waco, TX: Baylor University Press, 2018.

Dressler, Harold H. P. "The Identification of the Ugaritic Dnil with the Daniel of Ezekiel." *Vetus Testamentum* 29, no. 2 (Jan. 1979) 152–61. doi: https://doi.org/10.1163/156853379X00157.

Eagleton, Terry. *Literary Theory: An Introduction*. Minneapolis: University of Minnesota Press, 2008.

Elata-Alster, Gerda, and Rachel Salmon. "The Deconstruction of Genre in the Book of Jonah: Towards a Theological Discourse." *Literature and Theology* 3, no. 1 (Mar. 1989) 40–60. http://www.jstor.org/stable/23926662.

Erickson, Millard J. *Christian Theology*. 3rd ed. Grand Rapids: Baker Academic, 2013.

Eskenazi, Tamar Cohn. "Ezra: Name and Location in Canon." In *The New Oxford Annotated Bible: With the Apocrypha*, edited by Michael D. Coogan, 675–76. New York: Oxford University Press, 2018.

Eusebius. *The Church History*. Translated by Paul L. Maier. Grand Rapids: Kregel, 2007.

Faj, Attila. "The Stoic Features of the Book of Jonah." *Journal for Ancient Philosophy and Science* 12, no. 2 (Dec. 1978) 34–64. https://www.jstor.org/stable/40913415.

Bibliography

Gilderhus, Mark T. *History and Historians: A Historiographical Introduction.* 7th ed. Upper Saddle River, NJ: Pearson Education, 2010.

G., J. L. "Editorial: The Dialectic of Romans 13:1–7 and Revelation 13: Part Two." *Journal of Church and State* 19, no. 1 (Winter 1977) 5–20. https://www.jstor.org/stable/23914696.

Greer, Jonathan S., et al. *Behind the Scenes of the Old Testament: Cultural, Social, and Historical Contexts.* Grand Rapids: Baker Academic, 2018.

Harris, Laird R., et al. *Theological Workbook of the Old Testament.* Chicago: Moody, 1980.

Henderson, Leah. "The Problem of Induction." Stanford Encyclopedia of Philosophy Archive, Mar. 21, 2018. https://plato.stanford.edu/archives/sum2018/entries/induction-problem/.

Henderson, Suzanne W. "Authorship, Date, and Historical Context." In *The New Oxford Annotated Bible: New Revised Version with the Apocrypha*, edited by Michael D. Coogan, 1829–30. New York: Oxford University Press, 2018.

Jaffe, Richard M. "The Shin Sect of Buddhism." In *Selected Works of D. T. Suzuki*, edited by James C. Dobbins, 2:75–114. Oakland: University of California Press, 2015. http://www.jstor.org/stable/10.1525/j.ctt13x1gr5.

Jasper, Karl. *The Origin and Goal of History.* New York: Routledge Classics, 2021.

Köstenberger, Andreas J., and Richard D. Patterson. *Invitation to Biblical Interpretation: Exploring the Hermeneutical Triad of History, Literature, and Theology.* Grand Rapids: Kregel, 2011.

Law, Stephen. *Philosophy: History, Ideas, Theories, Who's Who, How to Think.* New York: Dorling Kindersley, 2007.

"The Leon Levy Dead Sea Scrolls Digital Library." Israel Antiquities Authority, n.d. https://www.deadseascrolls.org.il/home.

Lemon, M. C. *Philosophy of History: A Guide for Students.* New York: Routledge, 2003.

Martin, Lee Roy. *Introduction to Biblical Hebrew.* 4th ed. Cleveland, TN: CPT, 2018.

Matthews, Victor H., and Don C. Benjamin. *Old Testament Parallels: Laws and Stories from the Ancient Near East.* 3rd ed. Mahwah, NJ: Paulist, 2006.

Mayor, Adrienne. *The First Fossil Hunters: Dinosaurs, Mammoths, and Myth in Greek and Roman Times.* Princeton, NJ: Princeton University Press, 2011.

Merrill-Willis, Amy C. "Daniel: Historical Context, Composition, and Canonic Status." In *The New Oxford Annotated Bible: New Revised Version with Apocrypha*, edited by Michael D. Coogan, 1249–50. New York: Oxford University Press, 2018.

———. "Daniel: Name and Location in Canon." In *The New Oxford Annotated Bible: New Revised Version with Apocrypha*, edited by Michael D. Coogan, 1249. New York: Oxford University Press, 2018.

Metzger, Bruce. *The Canon of the New Testament: Its Origin, Development, and Significance.* New York: Oxford University Press, 1987.

———. *The New Testament: Its Background, Growth, and Content.* Nashville: Abingdon, 2003.

Bibliography

Miller, Robert J. *Helping Jesus Fulfill Prophecy*. Cambridge, UK: Lutterworth, 2016. https://www.jstor.org/stable/j.ctt1p5f2t4.7.

Minter, Deborah. "Facts of the Black Swan." Owlcation, July 11, 2020. https://owlcation.com/stem/Facts-of-the-Black-Swan.

Osborne, Grant R. *The Hermeneutical Spiral: A Comprehensive Introduction to Biblical Interpretation*. Downers Grove, IL: InterVarsity, 2006.

Paine, Thomas. *The Age of Reason*. New York: Barnes & Noble, 2006.

Paret, Peter. "Clausewitz." In *Makers of Modern Strategy: From Machiavelli to the Nuclear Age*, edited by Peter Paret et al., 186–213. Princeton, NJ: Princeton University Press, 1986.

Pelli, Moshe. "The Literary Art of Jonah." *Hebrew Studies* 20–21 (1979–1980) 18–28. https://www.jstor.org/stable/27908645.

Peterson, Michael, et al. *Reason and Religious Belief: An Introduction to the Philosophy of Religion*. New York: Oxford University Press, 2009.

Plantinga, Alvin. *God, Freedom, and Evil*. Grand Rapids: Eerdmans, 1977.

———. *Knowledge and Christian Belief*. Grand Rapids: Eerdmans, 2015.

Roden, Chet. *Elementary Biblical Hebrew: An Introduction to the Language and Its History*. San Diego: Cognella Academic, 2017.

Sáenz-Badillos, Angel. *A History of the Hebrew Language*. New York: Cambridge University Press, 1996.

Schniedewind, William M., and Joel H. Hunt. *A Primer on Ugaritic: Language, Culture, and Literature*. New York: Cambridge University Press, 2007.

Schreiner, Thomas R. *The King in His Beauty: A Biblical Theology of the Old and New Testaments*. Grand Rapids: Baker Academic, 2013.

Scott, David R. "The Book of Jonah: Foreshadowings of Jesus as the Christ." *BYU Studies Quarterly* 53, no. 3 (2014) 160–80. https://www.jstor.org/stable/43040012.

Smith, Mark S. "Ugarit and the Ugaritians." In *The World around the Old Testament: The People and Places of the Near East*, edited by Bill T. Arnold and Brent A. Strawn, 139–67. Grand Rapids: Baker Academic, 2016.

Starling, David I. *Hermeneutics as Apprenticeship: How the Bible Shapes Our Interpretive Habits and Practices*. Grand Rapids: Baker Academic, 2016.

Steele, Joel. *Early Christianity and Historical Methods: Repudiating the Contemporary Approach*. Eugene, OR: Resource, 2021.

———. *Philosophy of War: A Brief Analysis on Principles and Justifications*. Eugene, OR: Resource, 2020.

Timmer, Daniel. "Jonah's Theology of the Nations: The Interface of Religious and Ethnic Identity." *Revue Biblique* 120, no. 1 (Jan. 2013) 13–23. https://www.jstor.org/stable/44092183.

Tull, Patricia K. "Rhetorical Criticism and Intertextuality." In *To Each His Own Meaning: An Introduction to Biblical Criticisms and Their Application*, edited by Steven L. McKenzie and Stephen R. Haynes, 156–80. Louisville, KY: Westminster John Knox.

Wallace, Daniel B. *Greek Grammar: Beyond the Basics*. Grand Rapids: Zondervan, 1996.

Bibliography

Walton, John H. *Ancient Near Eastern Thought and the Old Testament: Introducing the Conceptual World of the Hebrew Bible.* 2nd ed. Grand Rapids: Baker Academic, 2018.

———, and J. Harvey Walton. *The Lost World of the Israelite Conquest: Covenant, Retribution, and the Fate of the Canaanites.* Downers Grove, IL: InterVarsity, 2017.

Wilken, Robert L. *The Christians as the Romans Saw Them.* 2nd ed. New Haven, CT: Yale University Press, 2003.

Williams, Michael. *Basics of Ancient Ugaritic: A Concise Grammar, Workbook, and Lexicon.* Grand Rapids: Zondervan Academic, 2012.

Zakovitch, Yair. "Jonah: Authorship and Date." In *The New Oxford Annotated Bible: New Standard Revised Version with Apocrypha*, edited by Michael D. Coogan, 1319–20. New York: Oxford University Press, 2018.

Index

absolute war, 74–75
A/C model, 51–52, 55
Acts, Book of, 46
afterlife, ancient view of, 3
The Age of Reason (Paine), 68
Alter, Robert, 16
Amenhotep IV, Egyptian ruler, 13
Amida Buddha, 12–13
Amos, Book of, 22–23, 77
Ancient Hebrew writings, 3–4
Ancient world
    afterlife, view of, 3
    causation and, 2
    orthodoxy in, 30–34
    time, view of, 2–3
    See also Near Eastern ancient cultures
apocalyptic genres, 39–42
apologies, 72–73
Aqhat, 6–7, 17–19
Aramaic language, 26
Argument Triumphant, 51
atenism, Egyptian religion, 13–14
Athanasius, 57, 64
Augustine, Saint, 64
Axial Age, 4–5
Aztec culture, 10–11

Baal, 3, 7–9, 14, 16–17, 20
Baal Cycle, 6, 7
Bakhtin, Mikhail, 29–30
beasts, in Revelation, 41–42
biblical Hebrew. *See* Classical Biblical Hebrew
Blomberg, Craig, 60

Calvin, John, 51–52
Canaan, language of, 21
Canaanite psalm, 16, 77
Carlyle, Thomas, 32
Carson, D. A., 45–46
causation, ancient view of, 2
celestial creatures, 16
Chou, Abner, 46–47
Christian institutions, 81
Christian orthodoxy, 33–34, 57
Christian scholars, polemical theory, 3
Christian worldview, 3
Christology, defined, 43
Cicero, 49
Classical Biblical Hebrew
    background, 21–23
    intertextuality, 29–30
    orthodoxy, 30–31

Index

Classical Biblical Hebrew (*cont.*)
   revisions, 24
   Samaritan Pentateuch, 25–26
   structuralism, 28–29
   targums, 26–28
   textual transmission, 22–24
   translations, 26
   vowel letters, 21, 24
Clausewitz, Carl von, 74–77
Clifford, William K., 50, 54
cognitive cultural phenomenon, 9, 10–12
Confucius, 4
Constantine, 48
contextualization, 76
Copan, Paul, 72, 73, 75
Corinthians, First Book of, 44–45, 47, 61
Corinthians, Second Book of, 56
Craig, William Lane, 73
critical rationalism, 50–51
Cross, Frank Moore, 15

Dagan, the god, 14
Daniel, Book of
   Ezekiel and, 77
   Old Testament/Ugaritic parallels, 6–7, 17–20
   as prophecy and apocalyptic genres, 40–41, 42
Dead Sea Scrolls, 22, 24, 25n13, 62
Did God Really Command Genocide? (Copan & Flannagan), 72
Didymus the Blind, 57
Dionysus cult, 48

Eagleton, Terry, 59, 82
Early Christianity and Historical Methods (Steele), 44, 45
Egyptian culture, 10–11, 13
El, the god, 6–7, 14–15
elohim, root of the word, 6, 15
empiricists, 53
Erickson, Millard, 60
Exegetical Fallacies (Carson), 45

eyewitnesses, of miraculous explanations, 47–49, 69
Ezekiel, 6–7, 17–20, 77

fables, 1
faith, reason and, 49–56, 78
fideism, 50, 55–56
Flannagan, Matthew, 72, 73, 75
Flavius Josephus, 56–57
flood stories, 14, 16

Galatians, Book of, 44, 46–47
genres, of biblical literature, 38–39
Gilgamesh epic, 14
God/gods
   El, 6–7, 14–15
   elohim, 15
   existence of, 49, 51–53
   Old Testament depictions of, 6–9
   parallel culture and, 5–9
   Yahweh, 15, 16, 31
Goulder, Michael, 48–49
Greek Septuagint, 26, 62–63

Hebrew language, 21–23
Hellenistic culture, 3, 4–5
henotheism, 15–16
The Hermeneutical Spiral (Osborne), 27
Hermeneutics as Apprenticeship (Starling), 61
The Hermeneutics of the Biblical Writers (Chou), 46
Hippolytus, 41
historians, methods used, 32–33
historical-critical approach
   ancient literature, 33
   biblical cannons, 58
   miraculous claims, 47–48
   problem with, 56–58
   scripture, 14, 78–80
   sources, closest to time of the events, 58
   supernatural components, 43
   theological claims, 79–80

Index

Hume, David, 55

iconography, 13
inductive argument, 53–55
inferences, 54
intentionality, 29
"The Interpretation of Matthew 12:39, 40" (Barnes, et al.), 66
intertextuality, 29–30
Invitation to Biblical Interpretation (Köstenberger and Patterson), 45
Isaiah
    Baalism criticism, 3, 8, 20
    connection to New Testament, 27, 30–38, 42
    language of Canaan, 21
    targum of, 27

Jesus, genealogy of, 36
Job, Old Testament, 6, 7, 17
John, Gospel of, 25, 37–38
Jonah, prophet, 63–68
Josephus, Flavius, 56–57
Judah, language of, 21

Keret Legend, 6
Kierkegaard, Søren, 50
Kings, First Book of, 8
Kings, Second Book of, 21, 22–23, 67
knowledge, possessors of, 4
Koran, 69
Köstenberger, Andreas J., 45, 63
KTU (Ugarit—Ras Shamra tablets), 5, 14, 17, 17n50
Kuntillet 'Ajrud, Sinai, 15

Late Biblical Hebrew, 22
Lemon, M. C., 2
limited war, 74
literature
    genres, of Old/New Testaments, 66–68
    Jonah and, 62–65
    perspectives, 65–66

postmodern thought on, 59–60
theology and, 59–62
western morality, 68–77
Livy's History of Rome, 47–48
The Lost World of the Israelite Conquest (Walton), 72
Luke, Gospel of, 36
Luther, Martin, 13, 41
Lutheranism, 13

Mark, Gospel of, 27–28
Marx, Karl, 51
Masoretic Text (MT), 21, 26, 62
Matthew, Gospel of
    on faith, 49
    genealogy of Jesus, 36
    Isaiah and, 30
    Jonah and, 63, 66
    Paul and, 44–45, 47
Mayor, Adrienne, 9
Merenptah, Egyptian king, 6
Miller, Robert J., 64
modern perspective, 1–2, 33
Mohamad, 69
monotheism, 15
morality, western, 68–77
Moses, 13, 68–69
mythological creatures, 9–10
myths/mythical thinking, 1–3

The Nature of the Gods (Cicero), 49
Near Eastern ancient cultures
    literature and, 30, 71
    as polytheist, 4, 30–31
    of recording history, 33
    worldview of, 3–4
New Testament
    authors of, 26–27, 35–38
    Daniel's prophecy connections, 41
    Old Testament and, 61–62
    See also specific books such as, Galatians, Revelation, and Gospels
Nietzsche, Friedrich, 51

Index

Noah, Old Testament, 7, 14, 17, 65

Old Testament
   analysis of, 77
   atrocities committed, 69–77
   cannon of, 34–35
   chronology, 18–19, 27–28
   dating of books, 19, 23–24, 67
   God, depictions of, 8–9
   God, term for, 6–7
   Near East influence on, 3
   New Testament authors and, 61–62
   See also specific book by name, such as Isaiah, Job, Psalms
On War (Clausewitz), 74
orthodoxy
   in Ancient World, 30–34
   Bible as inspired by God, 57
   core principles, 81
   parallel culture and, 14
Osborne, Grant, 27–28, 79

Paine, Thomas, 68–69
Paleo-Hebrew script, 24, 26
parallel cultural phenomenon
   disputes and fragmented conclusions, 14–20
   gods and characters, 5–9
   modern literature, 11–12
   mythological creatures, 9–10
   pyramids, 10–11
parallels in scripture, 42
Paret, Peter, 75
Patterson, Richard D., 45, 63
Peter, Second Book of, 46
Philippians, 62
philosophy of religion, 33–34
Phoenician writing system, 21–22
Plantinga, Alvin, 51–53, 55
Plato, 4
Pliny, 56
polemical theory, 3
polytheism, 15
polytheist cultures, 4, 30–31

possessor of knowledge, 4
postmodern thought, 9, 59–60
Practical Criticism (Richards), 11
prophecy genres, 39–42
Proto-Canaanite writing system, 22
Psalms, Book of
   Baal, hymn to, 8, 16–17
   Canaanite psalm and, 16, 77
   God, riding on the clouds, 8
   John's Gospel and, 37
   text usage, 22
pyramids, 10–11

Qumran. *See* Dead Sea Scrolls

rationalism, 50
reason, faith and, 49–56, 78
relativism, 70–72
religion, philosophy of, 33–34
Revelation, Book of, 40–42
Richards, I. A., 11–12
Romans, Book of, 42, 46
Rufinus, 57

Samaritan Pentateuch (SP), 25–26
Scott, David Randall, 65–66
scripts, ancient, 26, 83
scripture
   cannons in, 34–35, 57–58
   errors in, 60
   historical-critical approach to, 78
   human connections with, 81–82
   as inspired by God, 43–44, 57–58, 78–79
   message of, 78
   Old/New connections, 35–38
   parallels in, 42
   variations within, 80
   See also New Testament; Old Testament
secularism, 57
Semitic languages
   Hebrew, 21
   Ugaritic, 22
   West Semitic script, 83

Index

sensus divinitatis, 51, 55
Septuagint, 26, 62
Shin Buddhism, 12–13
Shinran (Buddhism sect founder), 12
Smith, Mark, 5–6
social and political objectives for humanity, 79
spiritual thinking, Axial Age shift to, 4–5
Sprinkle, Joe, 75
Starling, David, 61
strong rationalism, 53
structural features, similarities of, 10–11
structuralism, 28–29
Suzuki, D. T., 12

Tacitus, 56
Tale of Aqhat, 6
targums, 26–28
Teotihuacan culture, 10
theological influences
    apocalyptic genres, 39–42
    connections to Old/New testaments, 35–38
    genres, of biblical literature, 38–39
    historical methods of recording history, 32–34
    history, in terms of divine plan, 79–80

Old Testament cannon, 34–35
parallels in scripture, 42
prophecy genres, 39–42
textual analysis, 43–49
Thessalonians, First Book of, 44
Thomas Aquinas, Saint, 51, 64
Thucydides, 39
time, ancient view of, 2–3
Timothy, Second Book of, 43, 44, 46, 47
Torah, 25
A Treatise of Human Nature (Hume), 55

Ugaritic literature
    analysis of, 77–78
    Daniel in, 6–7, 17–20, 77
    deities, list of, 5
    documents, 22
    KTU text, 14
Ugarit—Ras Shamra (tablets), 5

Walton, John, 70–72, 75
war and conquests, 69–77
West Semitic scripts, 83
worldviews, cultural differences, 1–4
writing, discovery of, 82

Yahweh
    as one true God, 16, 31
    original name for, 15
    portrayal of, 31

www.ingramcontent.com/pod-product-compliance
Lightning Source LLC
Chambersburg PA
CBHW070934160426
43193CB00011B/1685